Rita Yi Man Li

Law, Economics and Finance of the Real Estate Market

A Perspective of Hong Kong and Singapore

Springer

Rita Yi Man Li
Sustainable Real Estate Research Center
Department of Economics and Finance
Hong Kong Shue Yan University
Hong Kong
Hong Kong SAR

This book project is supported by research grant offered by Hong Kong Shue Yan University.

ISSN 2191-5504 ISSN 2191-5512 (electronic)
ISBN 978-3-642-54244-2 ISBN 978-3-642-54245-9 (eBook)
DOI 10.1007/978-3-642-54245-9
Springer Heidelberg New York Dordrecht London

Library of Congress Control Number: 2014931396

Printed on acid-free paper

Springer is part of Springer Science+Business Media (www.springer.com)

Contents

Chapter 1
Law, Economics and Finance Issues in Singapore's Housing Development Board Flats

Abstract Housing a huge population in a small area is and has always been a difficult issue. Unlike other cities such as Hong Kong, the Singapore government plays a very active role in the provision of public housing. This chapter reviews the development of the housing development board's (HDB) residential estates, and the legal, economic, sustainability and finance issues of the HDB. Finally, case studies on Toa Payoh, 662 Buffalo Road in Little India and the Pinnacle are included in this chapter.

Keywords Residential market · Sustainable buildings · Finance · Housing law · Singapore

1.1 The Birth of the Housing Development Board

Since the 1920s, the population (approximately 1,100,000, many of whom were undocumented) grew at the dangerous Malthusian rate of 4.4 % per annum. In 1927, worried about the overcrowded urban areas, the colonial Government established the Singapore Investment Trust. The SIT planned roads and open spaces, constructed lanes between the back-to-back houses and built new dwellings to clear the slums. Approximately 2,000 housing units were built before World War II, and the first new town was in Tiong Bahru. In 1947, 72 % of the population resided in Singapore's central district. The population density reached 50,200 people per square kilometre, i.e., 2,500 people per square hectare. A family of seven could be crowded into a small cubicle, partitioned from the next family of seven by a frayed piece of sacking. Many of these people were forced to sleep on the floor, play and eat on the five-foot area, packed into a rabbit-warren of deep shophouses with limited ventilation through the air wells or windows. These slum dwellers were trapped in over-priced tenements that were a breeding ground for crime, disease and political extremism. Many of the Singaporeans could not even afford these homes. Squatter colonies of wood, attap and zinc sprang up at Toa Payoh and Bendemeer Village as the only alternative to high rents. The population

R. Y. M. Li, *Law, Economics and Finance of the Real Estate Market*,
SpringerBriefs in Economics, DOI: 10.1007/978-3-642-54245-9_1,

of these types of settlements reached 300,000 in 1950. Goh Keng Swee, a young civil servant, reported in 1953–1954 that 73 % of the households in Singapore were living in below standard accommodations. The fertility rate per woman was 5.76 in 1960 (it is only 1.24 now), with continuous migration into the city from rural Singapore and from Malaya. Furthermore, because the unemployment rate was high, people found it difficult to pay rent even if there had not been a shortage of good housing. Tuberculosis accounted for one in six deaths on the island. Dysentery was rife where drinking water was unsafe, kitchens were shared, and sewerage was unreliable. Stagnant water was one of the major causes of malaria and dengue. By 1960, SIT had built 23,264 flats, and 20,129 flats had been provided by the Harbour Board, the City Council and other public bodies. Nonetheless, only 8.8 % of Singapore's 1.6 million people were accommodated in public housing (Reisman 2007).

As the successor to the SIT, the Housing and Development Board (HDB) was established in the Ministry of National Development (Reisman 2007; Pheng et al. 2012) in 1960 as part of Singapore's national development program to provide affordable housing (Ong et al. 2003; Pheng 1996; Ibrahim et al. 2005). In 1965, by the time that Singapore first gained independence, there was still an acute shortage of housing, and a massive public housing programme was designed to provide public housing for Singaporeans (Pheng 1996). The programme built 54,430 and 100,000 units of housing (housing 30 % of the population) in 1965 and 1970, respectively (Reisman 2007). Nevertheless, the culture shock was at first tremendous: some pig farmers moved in with their pigs, others were afraid to use the lift or the electricity (Reisman 2007). By the late 1980s, over 85 % of Singapore's population was housed in HDB flats (Pheng 1996). Over the past four decades, 902,848 units of housing have been built to house some 86 % of Singapore's population. The HDB flats can be bought through direct allocation from the HDB as well as through the 'HDB resale market' (Ong et al. 2003). In 2005, the HDB built 879,566 units (50,103 rented, 829,463 owned by the HDB). The HDB also plans for comprehensive and coordinated communities and designs estates and new towns: car parks, playgrounds, libraries, swimming pools, shopping and eating facilities all form part of the design (Reisman 2007). In the following sections, the author explores the issues of finance, law and economics in the context of the sustainable housing sector in Singapore (Fig. 1.1, Table 1.1).

1.2 HDB Upgrading Programme

Quality furnishings and fittings are important to all the housing residents (Li and Chau 2010). As the quality of new housing projects improved, the quality gap between the old and new projects widened. To bridge the quality gap (Pheng et al. 2012), the Main Upgrading Programme (MUP) policy was introduced in 1989 with a pilot phase consisting of six precincts to be upgraded (Ho et al. 2009). In view of the overwhelming grassroots and residential support, the MUP policy per se was

Fig. 1.1 History of upgrading illustrated in the HDB hub (author's photo)

Table 1.1 Public housing sector development history in Singapore

Year	Key milestone
1920	Population grew at a fast rate of 4.4 %
1927	Singapore Investment Trust (SIT) was established to build public housing
1947	Population density reached 2,500 people per square hectare
1953–1954	73 % of the population live in below standard housings
1960	Housing Development Board (HDB) was established to replace SIT. 8.8 % of Singaporean lived in HDB housing (23,264 flats were built)
1965	Singapore gained independence. HDB had built 54,430 flats
1970	30 % of Singaporean lived in public housing. 100,000 flats were built
Late 1980	Over 85 % of Singaporean were housed in public housing
2005	879,556 housing units were built

officially launched in 1992 (Ho et al. 2009) as a major public housing policy to transform the HDB precincts that were over 20 years old into better quality housing. Older HDB housing estates such as Bishan and Pasir Ris were renovated to bring them closer to the quality of the new HDB housing estates (Pheng 1996; Ho et al. 2009; Pheng et al. 2012) if at least 75 % of the HDB households in the selected precinct opted for the upgrading during a polling exercise (Ho et al. 2009). In the 1990s, a series of 'upgrading' exercises were introduced by the HDB in addition to MUP: the Neighbourhood Renewal Programme (NRP), the Lift Upgrading Programme (LUP), and the Selective En Bloc Redevelopment Scheme (SERS) (Pheng et al. 2012). To position itself as a global city, these upgrading exercises in many

HDB estates have signalled a change in the function of public housing. These transformations are part of a larger process of social transformation in terms of housing policy, class and social mobility, governance, and community value systems (Goh 2001) that can prevent older estates from degrading into slums.

1.3 Recent Singapore HDB Development

In recent years, the expectations of Singaporeans in quality of housing have increased; the HDB's primary objective has been changed from the provision of basic housing to the provision of quality housing. Most of the dwellings are constructed with pre-cast technology. The HDB Heartware Forum, a series of discussions, consult the public and garner feedback and suggestions from Singaporeans regarding how to "enhance the precinct" and meet the needs and changing circumstances of the population's growing aspirations (Pheng et al. 2012). An information system for public housing management was also adopted to perform multiple tasks, which include online transactions for service charges, an inventory of physical properties, and the study of social and physical environments (Yu and Han 2001) (Figs. 1.2, 1.3 and 1.4).

In terms of appearance, the private dwellings usually have fences, but the HDB units do not.

1.4 Legal Issues in HDB

1.4.1 Quality Living Standard

In 1988, the enactment of the Town Councils Act decentralised the estate management of the HDB to the town councils, including the estate management work such as routine and cyclical maintenance and repair work (Pheng et al. 2012). The Housing Development Board (HDB) is empowered under the HDB Act (Cap. 129) Revised Edition 1997 (Hui et al. 2004). In 2000, the revised Town Councils Act stated that the mission of the various town councils was to provide a high quality physical living environment for the residents. The functions of the town council include finance and investments, estate improvement and maintenance, tenders and contracts and community relations (Pheng et al. 2012).

1.4.2 Restrictions on Ownership and Sales in HDB

Similar to any other real estate product, the prices of HDB resale flats are affected by supply, demand, the availability of close substitutes and the distance to various transportation nodes and activity centres (Ibrahim et al. 2005). Due to rapid

Fig. 1.2 Many choices for wall and floor tiles are available in the HDB Hub (author's photo)

Fig. 1.3 There is no fence in most of the HDB flats (author's photo)

Fig. 1.4 There is fence in the private residential housing in Paya Lebar (author's photo)

economic growth and the liberalisation of rules in the resale of HDB flats, the resale market is very active (Ong et al. 2003). Compared to the resale units, flats bought directly from the HDB are cheaper and there are more restrictions on income of the applicants. In recent years, the HDB regulates the eligibility and creditworthiness of prospective buyers. Various rules have been put in place to curb speculative activity; for example, a capital gains tax was implemented. These changes mark a shift in the residential market from being focused on bricks and mortar to being a contributing source to the further development of the financial sector (Phang 2001) (Fig. 1.5, Table 1.2).

1.5 HDB Finance

The central provident fund (CPF) is a fully funded, pay-as-you-go social security scheme that requires mandatory contributions by both employers and employees of a percentage of the employees' monthly contractual wage toward his/her account in the fund (Phang 2001). The use of the CPF in settling the down payment has also been changed accordingly. Homebuyers are allowed to use their CPF account to cover 50 % of the down payment amount, which is equal to 5 % of the property value, rather than the 10 % allowed before the policy change in July 2005. In addition, for those who are eligible for HDB loans at a concessionary interest rate, the repayment term for an HDB flat can be as long as 65 years minus the age of the

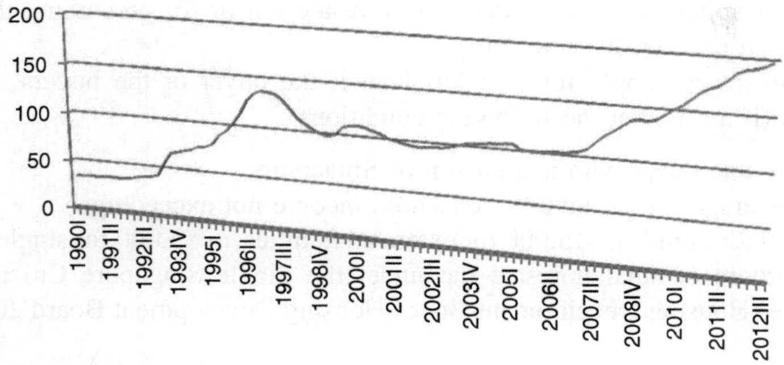

Fig. 1.5 Resale price index of HDB flats from the 1st quarter of 1990 to the 3rd quarter of 2012 (Housing Development Board 2012)

Table 1.2 A Comparison between HDB and private properties in Singapore (Hui et al. 2009)

HDB	Private properties
1. Residents need to physically occupy the HDB flat for a minimum occupation period before selling on the resale market (5 years for new HDB flats and 2.5 years for resale flats)	1. Freely transferable in the market
2. Mortgage loans can be obtained from either the HDB at concessionary rates for eligible applicants or from banks licensed by the Monetary Authority of Singapore at market rates since 1 Jan 2003	2. Mortgage loans obtained from banks or other financial institutions at market rates only
3. Home purchaser can use CPF of up to 5 % of the property price to pay for an HDB flat	3. CPF arrangements is the same as the purchase of HDB flats
4. 10 % down payment since 19 July 2005	4. 10 % down payment since 19 July 2005
5. Mortgage term depends on the applicants' age for the HDB concessionary loans	5. Approximately 30–35 years for private bank loans
6. After the resale of the HDB flats if one has enjoyed two subsidies, a resale levy required. Otherwise, no resale levy is needed	6. No resale levy is required
7. Income ceilings are subject to the size of the flat for new HDB flats. There is no income ceiling in the purchase of resale flats	7. There is no income ceiling

applicant. Because the minimum age for an applicant is 21 years, the repayment term under this policy can be as long as 44 years (Hui et al. 2009; Housing Development Board 2012). The HDB required that all potential flat buyers and transferees who wish to get an HDB concessionary loan first obtain an HDB Loan Eligibility (HLE) letter as of 1 Jan 2007. This letter must be obtained before the purchase or transfer of a flat and provides information on loan eligibility, monthly instalments, an indication of the loan amount for which the homebuyers are eligible and the amount of CPF in their account. The HDB will also work out the financial plan for the net loan at the point of (a) selecting a new flat for purchase,

(b) the first appointment for purchasing a resale flat or (c) processing the application for an existing flat transfer.

Flat buyers can apply for an HDB loan if the buyer or the buyers' essential occupiers (if any) meet the following conditions:

1. At least one buyer who is a citizen of Singapore;
2. Have average gross monthly household income not exceeding;
3. $10,000 for families, $15,000 for extended families, or $5,000 for singles buying a five-room or smaller resale flat under the Single Singapore Citizen (SSC) scheme (Housing Development Board Housing Development Board 2012).

The cut-off dates for the different types of transactions for a residential unit and the due date to obtain the HLE letter are summarised in the table below (Tables 1.3 and 1.4, Fig. 1.6).

1.5.1 Recent Development of HDB Finance

The HDB no longer offers market-rate mortgage loans to others since 1 Jan 2003. Mortgage loans may be obtained from banks and other financial institutions with a repayment term between 30 and 35 years (Hui et al. 2009; Housing Development Board 2012). Besides, the down payment rate in Singapore was adjusted downward from 20 to 10 % of the property price on the 19 July 2005 (Phang 2001).

1.6 The Housing Sector and the Economy in Singapore

The construction sector's fluctuations were a leading indicator of fluctuations in the GDP. Public housing activities also act as a macroeconomic stabiliser. In Singapore, the HDB sector has been used as a pump-timing device to create employment and income whenever a recession loomed, for example during 1975–1976 and 1982–1983. Nevertheless, the acceleration of public housing construction in 1982–1983 was considered to be excessive because it contributed to the 'overheating' of the economy in 1985–1987. The subsequent deceleration in HDB construction was also considered to be ill-timed because it coincided with a decline in private sector construction and a slow down in economic activity (Phang 2001).

1.7 Sustainable HDB Flats

Discussion on environment and its impact upon human beings has been a popular topic ever since Hippocartes and Aristotle times (Li 2009). Over 30 years since the 1973 energy crisis and 15 years since we became aware of man-made climate change, climate change has become a more severe global challenge. Global

Table 1.3 Cut-off dates for the HLE Letter (Housing Development Board 2012)

Type	Cut-off dates for cases that require an HLE letter
Purchase of new flats from HDB	
Completed/Uncompleted flat (under the walk-in selection, the balloting exercise and build-to-order system)	Booking of new flats on or after 1 Jan 2007
Purchase of resale flats	
Purchase of resale flat with/without CPF housing grant	Resale application received on or after 1 Jan 2007
Taking over ownership of an existing flat	
Taking over ownership of an existing flat	Application to take over the flat ownership by transfer received on or after 1 Jan 2007
Purchase of SERS replacement flat	
Purchase of replacement flat by SERS flat owners	Booking of replacement flats by SERS flat owners at SERS sites announced on or after 1 Jan 2007
Purchase of flats under the design, build and sell scheme	
Flats developed by a private developer and sold under the design, build and sell scheme	Booking of DBSS flats on or after 1 Jan 2007

Table 1.4 Type of CPF for different applicants (Housing Development Board 2012)

Target recipient	Type of CPF grant
For married couples who are first-time applicants	Family Grant
For married couples who are first-time applicants and buying a resale flat near their parents'/married child's HDB flat or owner-occupied private residential property	Higher-tier family grant
Applicants of $30,000 Family Grant/$40,000 Higher-Tier Family Grant, if • they have worked for at least 1 year and • their average monthly household income over the last year does not exceed $5,000	Additional CPF Housing Grant (AHG)
For single citizens: • Single applicants aged 35 and above who buy the resale flat to live on their own under the Single Singapore Citizen (SSC) Scheme • 2–4 Single Citizens aged 35 and above who jointly buy a resale flat under the Joint Singles Scheme (JSS) Married Singapore citizens aged 21 and above who are buying a resale flat under the non-citizen spouse scheme	Singles grant
For single citizens who are aged 35 years and above buying a resale flat to live with their parents	Higher-tier singles grant
For singles grant recipients who subsequently get married Also applicable to Singles Grant recipients under the Non-citizen spouse scheme whose non-citizen spouse or child subsequently obtain Singapore citizenship or permanent residence status	Top-up grant to the family grant
For first-time citizens with a spouse who had previously enjoyed a housing subsidy	Half-housing grant

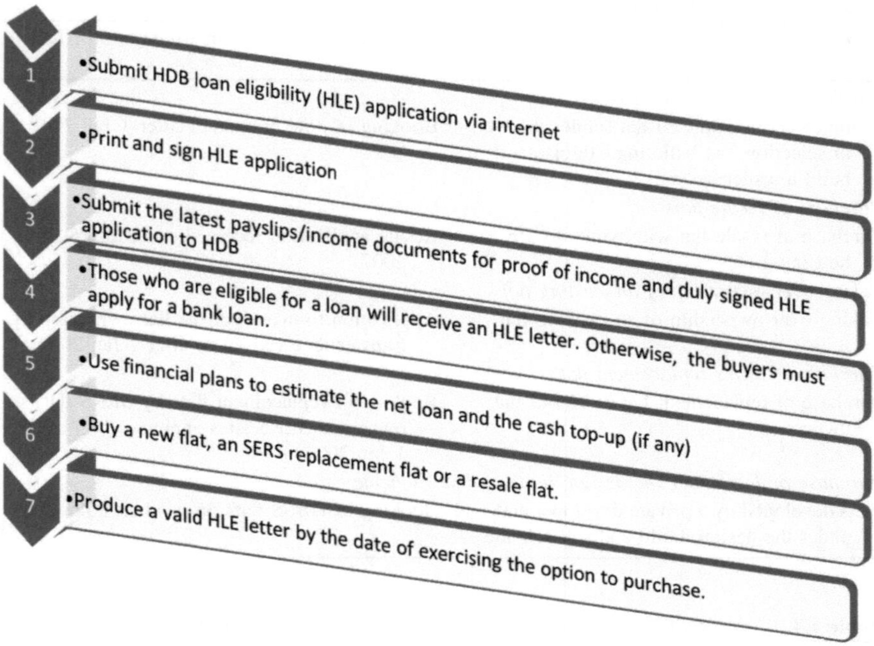

Fig. 1.6 Application for HDB loan eligibility letter (Housing Development Board 2012)

warming has drawn the attention of conservancy groups, economic theorists, population analysts, politicians and educators in the world. The construction sector has started to address the need for energy efficient buildings (Gething and Bordass 2006; Li and Ah Pak 2010; Li 2013; Bynum et al. 2013). Home automation, where systems are capable of automating a home via safety, energy management and communication elements, allows more efficient energy use and thereby contributing to sustainable development (Nazabal et al. 2012). In urban planning, communicative planning suggests that sustainable development lies in the possibility of the general public empowered by planning legislation to make comments on planning proposals, offering constructive suggestions to better shape the environment (Lai et al. 2009). In logistics, the industry has started to consider resources and environmental issues (Zheng and Zhang 2010). Discussion on sustainable development took place in the United Nations Conference on Environment and Development in 1992 (Li 2010a). And the notion of development should meet the needs of present generation without depriving the needs of the future generations has gained importance (Li 2010b, 2011). Apart from economic consideration, modern building envelop stresses the importance of sustainable development. There are three major dimensions in sustainable HDB housing development: environmental, social and economic. Although the idea of sustainable development is in the lips of many (Li and Ah Pak 2010), there is still a lack of low-energy buildings or systems in buildings that accurately report energy

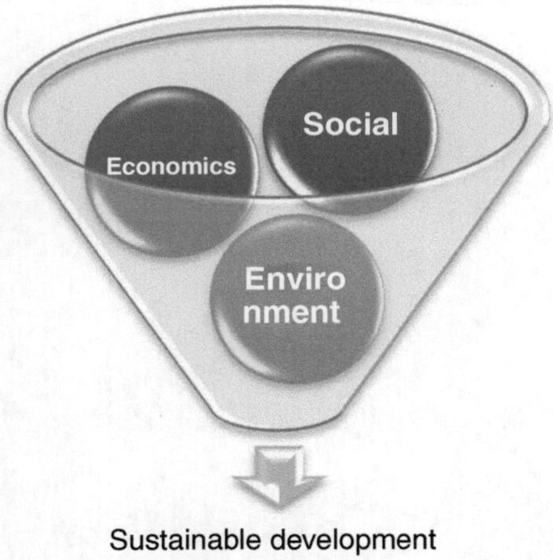

Fig. 1.7 Major constituent in sustainable development (Li 2011)

Fig. 1.8 Sustainable HDB flats in Singapore include environmental, social and economic dimensions

performance (Gething and Bordass 2006). Moreover, the new generations of high performance green buildings have not yet met their fullest potential. By applying sustainable techniques and methods over a period of time, environmental impacts can be substantially reduced both in the built environment and on a larger ecological scale (Bynum et al. 2013). The newly built sustainable housing units hope to perform as green estates by promoting recycling, saving energy and harvesting rainwater (Figs. 1.7, 1.8, 1.9, 1.10 and 1.11).

Fig. 1.9 Key thrusts in HDB's sustainable development: planning for evolving needs, design to construction to maintenance, research and development, engaging the community (author's photo)

Fig. 1.10 Innovations in sustainable development: greening the estates, harvesting rainwater, promoting recycling, saving energy (author's photo)

Fig. 1.11 Vertical garden in some of the HDB buildings (author's photo)

1.8 Case Studies

In this chapter, case studies are used to study the Singapore HDB. Case studies enables researcher to obtain in-depth information from observed behaviors and detailed descriptions of events. Case study refers to an intensive research of a single individual or event with an in-depth descriptive record (usually kept by an individual or group of individuals) (Li and Poon 2013). Typical data collected include interviews and observations (Li 2006). Although the its major problem lies in the breadth of study, a case study can be so unique that it may enhance the validity of the findings (Li and Poon 2013).

1.8.1 Case Study 1: Toa Payoh

Under the lens of Appold and Yuen (2007), the HDB areas "are walking environments. Social and commercial services are near residences. A small provision shop and a coffee shop are likely to be within a minute or two by walkways which are often covered to protect against the rain and midday sun. Neighbourhood shopping areas with food markets, food courts, medical and dental practices, a range of small shops and community centres are often within a 5-min walk. Primary and secondary schools are sprinkled throughout the new towns."

Fig. 1.12 184 Toa Payoh (old style of housing) (author's photo)

When the author asked for the best place to have a look at the local HDB, without hesitation, the HDB staff pointed to Toa Payoh. In fact, Toa Payoh is one of the earliest places where the HDB built the residential housing units to solve the squatter problem in Singapore. It is the best place to understand more about HDB development because it contains both old and new estates. The local residents told the author that the old buildings are those with a few storeys while the newer ones are skyscrapers. Its town centre has a library, cinemas, coffee shops, a park, an MTR station, a shopping arcade and a hawker centre. The area bustles with activity and is a wonderful place to soak up the local lifestyle. Visitors and locals have extensive choices, with a range of entertainment, merchandise and food options available. Here, visitors can pick up garments at attractively low prices, including T-shirts and shorts, and they can have a cheap lunch in the food court (Newasia-singapore.com 2013) (Figs. 1.12, 1.13, 1.14 and 1.15).

1.8.2 Case Study 2: Little India (662 Buffalo Road)

Singapore has one of the lowest crime rates in the world. A local resident comments that "many tourists misunderstood that a place like Little India with lots of Indians is not safe. It is absolutely wrong. It is as safe as any other place in Singapore… There is no security guard in many of the estates, you can stroll around the estates without any barrier." The estate at 662 Buffalo Road is a HDB

Fig. 1.13 Newer style of housing in Toa Payoh (author's photo)

Fig. 1.14 Shopping arcade in Toa Payoh (author's photo)

Fig. 1.15 Toa Payoh MTR station (author's photo)

estate near the Little India MRT station and many Indians live in this area. Many residents who live in 662 Buffalo Road, however, are Chinese. In this residential tower, there are two residential units on each floor. The current rent of this HDB unit is approximately S$3,100 for a fully furnished three bedroom units with 111.67 m^2 (Lim 2013). Compared to Toa Payoh and the later case study, "the Pinnacle", this housing estate contains more Indian shops and restaurants (Figs. 1.16, 1.17, 1.18, 1.19 and 1.20).

1.8.3 Case Study 3: The Pinnacle@Duxton

To position Singapore as a global city and to construct a possible space for increasing public input and expression, the HDB moved from a 'modern' to 'post-modern' architectural style (Goh 2001). One of the best examples of the post-modern HDB flats is Pinnacle@Duxton (hereafter the Pinnacle). This estate was chosen by the Council on Tall Buildings and Urban Habitat for the Best Tall Building Award—Asia and Australasia 2010. This award recognises projects that have made extraordinary contributions to the advancement of tall buildings, the urban environment, sustainability and building processes and/or innovations (Council on Tall Buildings and Urban Habitat 2010) (Fig. 1.21).

This estate is the first 50-storey public residential project in Singapore; it includes 1,848 apartments in 7 towering blocks. Born out of an international

Fig. 1.16 Little India (662 Buffalo Road)

design competition for public housing, the estate is also the first in the world with 2 unique skybridges that link the 7 blocks at the 26th and 50th storey. The sky-bridges create possibly the longest green skygardens in the world, offering panoramic views of the city (Pinnacle@Duxton 2013). Curved across its site, these buildings take the concept of "streets in the sky" to a new level, providing high-density living and a fascinating solution for how we can make the best use of that most precious of resources: land (Council on Tall Buildings and Urban Habitat Council on Tall Buildings and Urban Habitat 2010). The open green space also enhances the quality of urban life, benefits the urban environment and makes the city liveable (Yuen and Hien 2005). Furthermore, the building towers were constructed off-site, and the pre-fabricated units were delivered and assembled on-site. This style of construction not only reduces the construction time and costs, it also lowers wastage. An unprecedented choice of exterior façade treatments—bay windows, planter boxes, bays, windows, and balconies—provide a wide range of options that suit the varied tastes of Singaporeans. The entire project marries a

Fig. 1.17 There are two residential units on each floor

Fig. 1.18 Little India MRT station is within 2 min walk of the nearby public housing (author's photo)

Fig. 1.19 Pusat Tekka includes restaurants and shops for residents nearby (author's photo)

Fig. 1.20 An Indian restaurant downstairs in 662 Buffalo Road (author's photo)

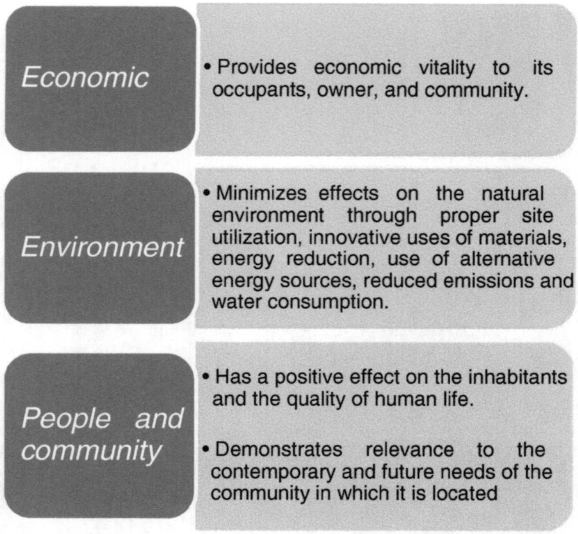

Fig. 1.21 Sustainable requirements for the Best Tall Building Award (Council on Tall Buildings and Urban Habitat 2010)

Fig. 1.22 The entrance of the Pinnacle (author's photo)

Fig. 1.23 Skybridges in residential towers of the Pinnacle (author's photo)

Fig. 1.24 Green space in the Pinnacle (author's photo)

Fig. 1.25 Balcony is available in some of the housing units, making it aesthetically special (author's photo)

Fig. 1.26 Lift lobby of the Pinnacle (author's photo)

Fig. 1.27 Outram Park station is close to the Pinnacle (author's photo)

private housing estate with public space, addresses social, financial pragmatic and even political issues (Council on Tall Buildings and Urban Habitat 2010).

According to the HDB staff, despite its relative high quality, the price to buy a flat in this HDB estate is approximately half the price of a nearby private estate. Therefore, there was keen competition for spaces among applicants. Priority was given to those who had lost the lottery for HDB flats more than once (Figs. 1.22, 1.23, 1.24, 1.25, 1.26 and 1.27).

1.9 Conclusion

The HDB in Singapore was established as a statutory authority to provide affordable housings to Singaporean. Public housing activities also act as a macroeconomic stabiliser as construction sector's fluctuations were a leading indicator of fluctuations in the GDP. The central provident fund offers help for those who are in needs of down payment. Although the HDB flats are sold at a substantial lower price as compared to those private ones, the three case studies show that the HDB provide ample facilities to residents. Shopping arcades, restaurants, shops are within walking distance.

References

Appold S, Yuen B (2007) Families in Flats, Revisited. Urban Stud 44:569–589

Bynum P, Raja F, Issa RA, Olbina S (2013) Building information modeling in support of sustainable design and construction. J Constr Eng Manage 139:24–34

Council on Tall Buildings and Urban Habitat (2010) The Pinnacle @ Duxton, Singapore. http://www.ctbuh.org/TallBuildings/FeaturedTallBuildings/Archive2010/ThePinnacleDuxtonSingapore/tabid/2283/language/en-US/Default.aspx. Accessed 12 Jan 2012

Gething B, Bordass B (2006) Rapid assessment checklist for sustainable buildings. Build Res Inf 34:416–426

Goh RBH (2001) Ideologies of 'upgrading' in Singapore public housing: post-modern style, globalisation and class construction in the built environment. Urban Stud 38:1589–1604

Ho DKH, Hui ECM, Ibrahim MFB (2009) Asset value enhancement of Singapore's public housing main upgrading programme (MUP) policy: a real option analysis approach. Urban Stud 46:2329–2361

Housing Development Board (2012) HDB InfoWEB Housing Development Board. http://www.hdb.gov.sg. Accessed 29 Dec 2012

Hui CME, Yu KH, Ho DKH (2009) Dynamics of assisted homeownership in Singapore. J Urban Aff 31:195–212

Hui ECM, Ho VSM, Ho DKH (2004) Land value capture mechanisms in Hong Kong and Singapore: a comparative analysis. J Prop Invest Financ 22:76–100

Ibrahim MF, Cheng FJ, Eng KH (2005) Automated valuation model: an application to the public housing resale market in Singapore. Prop Manage 23:357–373

Lai LWC, Lam G, Chau KW, Wong SK, Hung CWY, Li RYM (2009) Statutory zoning and the environment: a Hong Kong empirical analysis of the direct effect of zoning on the environment and the potential contribution of planning conditions to sustainable development. Prop Manage 27:242–266

Li RYM (2006) Effectiveness of various construction safety measures in Hong Kong real estate and construction. The University of Hong Kong, Hong Kong

Li RYM (2009) The impact of climate change on residential transactions in Hong Kong. J Built Human Environ Rev 2:11–22

Li RYM (2010a) Constructing sustainable vertical cities: strategies to enhance closer cooperation between ASEAN contractors on pollution problem under the lens of economic game theories, cost benefit analysis and dynamic Markov chain theories. Asian Soc Sci 6:10–18

Li RYM (2010b) Traditional Chinese mode of thinking, sustainable development and property management. Real Estate Dev Econ Res J 2:70–86

Li RYM (2011) Building our sustainable cities. Common Ground Publishing, Illinois

Li RYM (2013) The usage of automation system in smart home to provide a sustainable indoor environment: a content analysis in Web 1.0. Int J Smart Home 7:47–59

Li RYM, Ah Pak DH (2010) Resistance and motivation to share sustainable development knowledge by Web 2.0. J Inf Knowl Manage 9:251–262

Li RYM, Chau KW (2010) Constructing quality first hand dwellings in Hong Kong: a study of court cases in 2000–2008. Manchester

Li RYM, Poon SW (2013) Case studies on safety measures implementation. In: Li RYM, Poon SW (eds) Construction safety. Springer, Germany

Lim R (2013) For rent—662 Buffalo Road (D08). http://www.sgvicinity.com/12885358. Accessed 12 Jan 2013

Nazabal JA, Gómez J, Falcone F, Fernández-Valdivielso C, Branchi PE, Matías IR (2012) Android application for accessing KNX devices via IP connection. Int J Smart Home 6:39–46

Newasia-singapore.com (2013) Toa Payoh. http://www.newasia-singapore.com/places_to_go/suburban_living/toa_payoh_20070601120.html. Accessed 12 Jan 2013

Ong SE, Ho KHD, Lim CH (2003) A constant-quality price index for resale public housing flats in Singapore. Urban Stud 40:2705–2729
Phang SY (2001) Housing policy, wealth formation and the Singapore economy. Housing Stud 16:443–459
Pheng LS (1996) The management of large-scale upgrading programmes for public housing in Singapore. Prop Manage 14:27–32
Pheng LS, Deng X, Lye L (2012) Communications management for upgrading public housing projects in Singapore. Struct Surv 30:6–23
Pinnacle@Duxton (2013) The Pinnacle@Duxton. http://www.pinnacleduxton.com.sg/index.php. Accessed 11 Jan 2013
Reisman D (2007) Housing and superannuation: social security in Singapore. Int J Soc Econ 34:159–187
Yu SM, Han SS (2001) Information systems in public housing management: case study of a town council in Singapore. Facilities 19:233–239
Yuen B, Hien WN (2005) Resident perceptions and expectations of rooftop gardens in Singapore. Landscape Urban Plan 73:263–276
Zheng L, Zhang J (2010) Research on green logistics system based on circular economy. Asian Soc Sci 6:116–119

Chapter 2
Internalization of Environmental Externality in Dwellings: Review of Court Cases in Hong Kong in the Past Two Decades

Abstract In 1960, Ronald Coase suggested that there are many methods to solve the problem of externality apart from imposing Pigovian tax; internalization is one of those noted in relation to the Problem of Social Costs. This chapter studies the possibility of residents receiving their compensation from pollutant generators. Data collected from Hong Kong Law Reports over the past 20 years show that there has been a 40-fold increase in the number of water seepage court cases since the first case happened in 1994. The total amount of compensation has also increased substantially. There is, however, far fewer court cases related to residents seeking compensation from pollutant generators with regard to noise and air pollution. Possible reasons for this are the high transaction costs and low expected benefit derived from court cases.

Keywords Externalities · Pollution · Housing · Court cases · Hong Kong

2.1 Introduction

Environmental problems such as noise and air pollution often lead to health problems, for example, cardiovascular disease (White et al. 2011; Manu et al. 2012; The National Archives 2012), increased mortality rate (Manu et al. 2012), urinary system damage (Chockalingam and Sornakumar 2011), hearing impairment (Morantz 2009) or even psychological problems (Navon and Kolton 2006; Wadick 2010). The outbreak of Severe Acute Respiratory Syndrome (SARS) in Hong Kong was an example of the consequence of improper management of residential pipes and drainage systems. Possibly because of the side-effects on health, the impact of negative externality, e.g. noise (McGehee 2001; Theebe 2004) and air pollutants (Henning and Ridker 1967; Crocker 1971; Deyak and Smith 1974; Chattopadhyay 1999; Connor 2004) on property and rental value has been studied extensively. Environmental damage may be generated by individuals who inflict harm on those nearby, i.e. the costs are not borne by the pollutant generators. Damage caused by

R. Y. M. Li, *Law, Economics and Finance of the Real Estate Market*,
SpringerBriefs in Economics, DOI: 10.1007/978-3-642-54245-9_2,

water leakage from an upper floor, for example, can lead to visual problems in false ceilings or even structural problems in the ceilings of lower premises. Such "costs", generated by those who live on an upper floor, should be compensated in the world of zero transaction costs with property rights well-defined (each unit is bought and owned by somebody). Unfortunately, such utopian situation is difficult to be realized in view of the positive real world transaction costs. Even though individuals do not have incentives to misrepresent their own interests, comprehensive negotiations impose overwhelming costs (Baily 1993). In fact, strata-title ownership characteristics coupled with the dense habitation often ends up with building management disputes in Hong Kong, thereby disintegrating neighbourhood relationships. More importantly, such unresolved problems pose safety and health concerns for our community at large (Kirkwood and Lande 2008). This chapter sheds light on court cases available in Hong Kong Law Reports.

2.2 Market Externality, Private Property Rights and Transaction Costs

Pigou introduced the concept of externality in 1920 (Calvani 1982). Externality arises when the actions of an individual leads to a loss of wealth or utility of others (Roberts 1996). It can also be interpreted as the actions of one actor create costs or benefits for others which are not captured by contractual relationships (Meadowcroft 2004). It can either be negative or positive. The former case, as a subject matter in the law of tort, usually receives greater attention (Roberts 1996). For example, the release of methyl isocyanate in Bhopal led to many innocent people's deaths and injuries nearby (Li and Hung 2013). In case of positive externality, a major retailer may open in a previously quiet town centre street, bringing an increase trade to the shops nearby (Meadowcroft 2004). It therefore usually refers to the phenomenon where divergence exists between social and private costs (Calvani 1982). Whilst Pigovian welfare economics argues that the existence of externality is a case of market failure and government intervention is required to deal with negative externality (Anderson et al. 1998), Coase argues that if transaction costs between the two parties are low enough and private property rights (the right to own, use and exchange) are well-defined, people should be able to bargain for an efficient solution (Coase 1960; Roberts 1996; Li 2009). Under certain circumstances, market prices reflect how externality can be internalized (Table 2.1), as noted in Steven Cheung's paper on internalizing externality between traditional bee keepers and apple growers (Glofcheski 2009). In the case of pollution, the externality generators could pay victims a sum of money, leaving both parties better off (Roberts 1996). Alternatively, the source of pollutants can be removed from the parties affected (Coase 1960).

In Hong Kong's housing market, private property rights are well-defined in most premises. Ownership of one particular unit can be checked easily in the Land Registry (Takigawa 2009), so the market should be able to internalize

Table 2.1 The effect of negative externality on housing price reduction (Li 2013)

Types of noise pollution	Author	Relationship between pollutants and housing price	Country
PM10	Gonzalez et al. (2013)	One unit reduction in PM10 levels is valued at US $41.73 for Mexico City, 36.34 for Guadalajara and 43.47 for Monterrey respectively	Mexico
Total suspended particulates reduction in total suspended particulates results in a 0.2–0.4 % increase in mean housing values	Chay and US	Greenstone (2005)	1 mg/m^3
Sulphur	Ridker and Henning (1967)	There was a decrease in sulfation of 0.25 mg/100 cm^2/day would increase values of owner-occupied single-family homes by between $83 and $245	US
Particulate concentration and summer oxidant	Nelson (1978)	There was a decrease in $57.61 and $14.11 for particulates and oxidants respectively	US
pH value of the water	Epp and Al-Ani (1979)	There was an increase in a 5.9 % in the mean sales value of residential properties	US
Water quality	Young (1984)	The estimated decrease in worth due to poor water quality was approximately $4,200	US
PCB pollution	Mendelsohn et al. (1992)	Properties' value fell from $10,000 to $7,000	US
Landfill	Jauregui and Hite (2010)	There was 16 % lower price for a property which was closer to the landfill	US
Landfill	Nahman (2011)	Loss of value per property (R) relative to those 4 km away was R57,261.91 (1–2 km), R34,357.15 (2–3 km), R34,357.15 (3–4 km)	South Africa
Landfill	Ham et al. (2013)	Active landfills were positively significant related to property prices at 1 % level within 0–2 km. From 0 to 3 km, the coefficient was negative and statistically significant at the 1 % level of confidence. From 0 to 4 km, however, became statistically insignificant at the 10 % level of confidence	UK
Landfill	Nelson et al. (1992)	The landfill adversely affected home values in the range of 12 % at the landfill boundary and 6 % at about one mile. Beyond about 2–2.5 miles adverse effects are negligible	US

(continued)

Table 2.1 (continued)

Types of noise pollution	Author	Relationship between pollutants and housing price	Country
Traffic noise	Luttik (2000)	Properties price dropped by 5 %	Netherland
Traffic noise	Pennington et al. (1990)	Properties price lowered by 6 %	UK
Traffic noise	Taylor et al. (1982)	Residential price decreased by $312 per decibel in highway areas and $254 in arterial sites	Canada
Highway noise	Nelson (1982)	The noise led to a drop from 8 to 10 %	US
Highway noise	Gamble et al. (1974)	Dollar per decibel rate ranged from $60 to $646	US
Airport noise	Cohen and Coughlin (2009)	65-decibel noise contour was 7.5 % discount for semi-log model, i.e. $8,612 or 10.6 % for the linear specification In 70-decibel noise contour, there was a drop in 12.3 % ($14,330) or 17.7 %	US
Airport noise	Cohen and Coughlin (2007)	There was be a drop in 20.8 %	US
Airport noise	Baranzini and Jos (2005)	There was a drop in 1 %	Switzerland
Airport noise	Jon (2004)	There was a drop in 0.8–0.9 % in property value per decibel	Canada
Air quality and waste site	Thayer et al. (1992)	Every 6 % improvement in ozone had a value of approximately $3,841 in nominal dollars. Each additional mile from a waste site was $1,349 in the linear equation and $1,701 in the semi-log equation	The US

uncompensated effects in the absence of transaction costs (Anderson et al. 1998). Nevertheless, transaction costs exist in our real world: there are costs involved in identifying the source of pollutant generators and costs in identifying the possible problems. Indeed, transaction costs are one of the major factors which affect people's motivation to complain and one step ahead, to lodge complaints in court.

To illustrate the unique pollution problem in Hong Kong's concrete jungle, I will use Metro City as an example (note that it is only an example and the court cases that I found were not restricted to this estate only but were scattered around all the residential areas in Hong Kong). Metro City is one of the large-scale residential estates with 11 towers, 6–8 flats on each floor and densely populated environments can be found easily in Hong Kong. In the case of water seepage, it is quite easy to identify the source of pollutants as the one who lives in Flat H, 35/F, Tower 6 only needs to search the 3 units above (the highest one is 38/F), i.e. the H flats from 36/F to 38/F. As water seepage will not stop at a particular time, it is

Fig. 2.1 Floor plan of metro city phase 2 (11 towers are inside the *rectangle*) (Centaline Property Agency 2013)

quite easy to locate the source. Yet, in the case of noise pollution, it is quite difficult to identify the source of the pollution. First, the one who generates loud noise may be in Tower 2, Tower 10 or even in Yan Lan (the tower with 10 flats on each floor over 30 storeys in a circle). This implies that it is quite hard to find out where the defendant is. The same theory also holds true for some air pollution cases, such as bad smells. The second problem is that air and noise pollution generators may stop polluting at some time while water seepage cannot stop at any time once it has occurred. Therefore, the author hypothesizes that there should be a lot more water seepage cases which ultimately end up in the courts as the costs of identifying the source of pollutants are comparatively lower (Fig. 2.1).

2.3 Liability of Negative Environmental Externality Producer Under Common Law

Common environmental externality in dwellings, namely air pollution, noise and water leakage/seepage have different considerations when the judges made their judgments under common law in Hong Kong.

2.3.1 Air Pollution

Plaintiffs in Hong Kong may rely on "nuisance" to seek air pollution compensation in court (Westlands Estates Limited and Egremont Estates Limited v Swilynn (HK) Limited [1985]). Nuisance, according to the learned judge in Born Chief Co. (trading as Beijing Restaurant) v George Tsai and Another [1996], can be defined as "an act of omission which is an interference with, disturbance of or annoyance to, a person in the exercise or enjoyment of his occupation of land or of some right used or enjoyed in connection with land". In another court case Teng Fuh Co Ltd v Air pollution Board and another [2001], it is stated that "air pollutants defined in Sect. 2.2 of the Ordinance refers to 'any solid, particulate, liquid, vapour, objectionable odour or gaseous substance emitted into the atmosphere'. Smells that are objectionable may therefore constitute air pollutants".

2.3.2 Noise Pollution

In determining whether or not the "noise" constitutes pollution, judges do not only put their lens on Hong Kong court cases, legal rules and regulations; they may also consider cases and law from overseas which also rule under the umbrella of common law jurisdiction. For example, the judge in Step In Ltd v Noise Control Appeal Board and Another gave his judgment on Australian and UK law. In assessing "noise" he read a Code of Practice on Environmental Noise Control at Concerts 1995 in England which was issued by the Noise Council: "(a)ssessment of noise in terms of dB(A) is very convenient but it can underestimate the intrusiveness of low frequency noise. Furthermore, low frequency noise can be very noticeable indoors. Thus, even if the dB(A) guideline is being met, unreasonable disturbance may be occurring because of the low frequency noise. With certain types of events, therefore, it may be necessary to set an additional criterion in terms of low frequency noise, or apply additional control conditions." He further pointed out that "a criterion for nuisance which relies only on subjectivity represents an easy get-out for local authorities seeking to avoid a more difficult approach and is unjust. It has been my position for very many years that whilst indeed there are many situations where music noise should not be allowed to intrude into people's dwellings, an objective criterion is the only fair way of addressing the issue. All other sources of noise are measured objectively so why single out entertainment noise as the sole exception?" To decide whether the defendant is liable or not for noise pollution, the judge in Jack Gordon Leslie Smith and Another v Tam Wing Wah and Another [2007] stressed the importance of reasonableness, saying "Tams (defendant) should not be punished because the Smiths may have unreasonable expectations of silence, or at least quietness, within the confines of their home".

2.3.3 Water Seepage/Leakage

Similar to the abovementioned "reasonableness", judges in relation to water seepage/leakage also consider it as a major concern in determining remedies or compensation. The learned judge in Bulmer Ltd and Another v ACL Electronics (HK) Ltd [1991] pin pointed that where condensation occurred on plaintiff's ceiling the resulting damage was a consequence "within the general range which any reasonable person might foresee and was not of an entirely different kind which no one could anticipate and "the defendant's fault in relation to the causation or remoteness of the damages awarded or to the matters of which he took judicial notice".

Nevertheless, not all plaintiffs who win their case receive a monetary sum in compensation. In some cases, the judge restrains the defendant's activity to stop the source of negative externality, which is quite similar to Coase's idea in the Problem of Social Cost (Coase 1960). In Incorporated Owners of Jing Hui Garden v Ng Kei Sang [2007], the defendant was restrained from erecting or installing any pipes, other fittings or air-conditioners at the Building's external wall not provided for under the DMC.

2.4 Current Legal Rules and Regulations Concerning and Regulating the Problem of Externality in Residential Units

2.4.1 Air Pollution Regulations

The authorized officer or the Authority may take the followings into consideration: (1) the advice of the Director-General of Civil Aviation; (2) technical memorandum; (3) a medical practitioner's opinion; (4) the distance between the source of emission and the place which is affected; (5) the location of the place being affected; (6) the duration, frequency and time of the emission; (7) publications or research results which indicate that the emission may have adverse health effects; (8) any of the following effects which, in the opinion of the Authority or the authorized officer is contributed to or caused by emission: (1) the corrosion, staining of, or damage to equipment, plant, building or other material; (2) an objectionable odour; (3) irritation of the skin, nose or eye, or any other sensory discomfort; (4) the deposit of grit, particles or dust of any kind; (5) skin eye, nose irritation or any other sensory discomfort; (6) normal activities disturbance of by colour; (7) an authorized officer confirms that the emission may affect public safety; (8) any other effect which in the opinion of an authorized officer or the Authority is unreasonable for a member of the public to suffer.

Under s.10 of the Air Pollution Control Ordinance (Cap. 311) (the Ordinance), where an authorized person or the Authority is satisfied that air pollutants emitted from a polluting process is contributing to or causing air pollution which is imminent or exists, the Authority or the authorized officer may issue a verbal or written air pollution abatement notice to the person who carries out the activity and require him or the owner of the premises to abate or reduce or cease air pollutants emission or the polluting process. In Teng Fuh Co Ltd v Air pollution Board and another [2001], the learned judge provided an interpretation on the captioned piece of legislation; he said "in defining polluting process, s.2 referred to, inter alia, an activity and so, for there to be a polluting process, there had to be some activity by X".

2.4.2 Rules and Regulations on Noise

Neighbourhood noise includes noise produced in domestic premises by sources such as television sets, air-conditioners or dogs, and noise produced in public places by sources such as radios, hawkers or loudspeakers. Sections. 2.4 and 2.5 of the Noise Control Ordinance were designed specifically for this type of noise and came into operation on 1 November 1989. Section. 2.4 of the Ordinance controls noise which causes annoyance during holidays or at night from 11 p.m. to 7 a.m. Section 2.5 of the Ordinance controls particular noise sources at any time. These include games, musical instruments, animals and birds, loudspeakers, trades or businesses and air conditioners. Table 2.2 illustrates the types of noise offence and the corresponding fines and Fig. 2.2 sheds light on the warning, abatement notices, and summonses issued in 2008.

2.4.3 Rules and Regulations on Water Seepage/Leakage

To identify whether water seepage or leakage problems exist, there are three stages of tests in Hong Kong. In stage 1, health inspectors or environmental nuisance investigators have to confirm the extent of water seepage nuisance by visiting the complainant's premises. If the moisture content of seepage area is equal to or more than 35 %, and premises of other owner are suspected to have caused seepage, Joint Office staff will carry out stage 2 "initial investigation" with one or more of the following tests (Li 2013) (Table 2.3).

If the source of seepage cannot be identified after stage 2 "initial investigation", Joint Office will proceed to stage 3 "professional investigation". Building Safety Officers or staff of private consultants appointed by Joint Office will carry out one or more of the tests. In complicated cases, for instance, those having more than one seepage locations will have multiple visits for investigation and tests (Li 2013) (Table 2.4).

Table 2.2 Types of noise offenses and their corresponding fines (Environmental Protection Department 2011)

Noise control ordnance section(s)	Type of offence	Maximum fine
4, 5	Noise from domestic premises and public space (neighborhood noise)	$10,000
6, 7	Noise from construction sites	$10,000 on the first conviction, $200,000 on second or subsequent conviction plus $20,000 a day
13	Noise from places other than domestic premises, public places or construction sites (industrial noise)	
14–17	Noise from products	
13A	Noise from intruder alarm system in any premises	$10,000 and imprisonment for 3 months
13B	Noise from intruder alarm system in any vehicle	$10,000

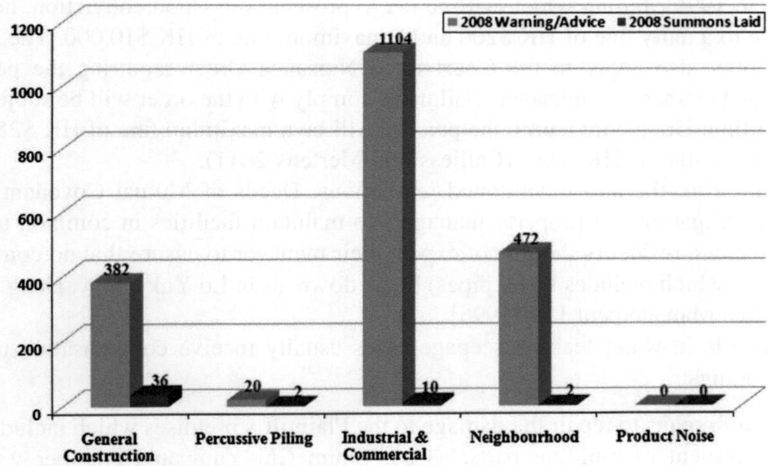

Fig. 2.2 Warning, abatement notices, summons laid in 2008 (Environmental Protection Department 2011)

Table 2.3 Test to be carried out in stage 2 (Li 2013)

Test method	Test location	Premises involved	Time required
Reversible pressure test	Water supply pipes and seepage area	Suspected premises and complainant's premises	About 3–5 h
Colour water test	Drainage outlets	Suspected premises	About 1 h
Moisture content monitoring	Wall surface/ceiling	Complainant's premises	About 0.5 h each time

Table 2.4 Test to be carried out in stage 3 (Li 2013)

Test method	Test location	Premises involved	Time required
Ponding test	Floor slabs of balcony/bathroom/ kitchen	Suspected premises	About 2 h
Reversible pressure test (if not carried out in stage II)	Water supply pipes and seepage area	Suspected premises and complainant's premises	About 3–5 h
Moisture content monitoring	Wall surface/ceiling	Complainant's premises	About 0.5 h each time

If the source of seepage is confirmed as a sanitary nuisance, the Joint Office set up by the Food and Environmental Hygiene Department and the Buildings Department may issue a nuisance notice under the Public Health and Municipal Services Ordinance (Cap. 132), directing the nuisance generator to fix the problem (Kovacic 1996), failing which will be led to prosecution. Upon conviction, he/she is liable to a daily fine of HK $200 and a maximum fine of HK $10,000. The Joint Office may also apply to the Court for a Nuisance Order requiring the person concerned to abate the nuisance. Failure to comply with the order will be subject to prosecution. Upon conviction, the penalty will be a maximum fine of HK $25,000 and a daily fine of HK $450 (Calliess and Mertens 2011).

Apart from the abovementioned regulations, Deeds of Mutual Covenant also impose obligations on property managers to maintain facilities in common areas. Nevertheless, residents should not expect their manager to ensure that no common facilities (which includes water pipes) break down, as in Lo Yuk Chu v. Hang Yick Properties Management Ltd [1996].

Plaintiffs in water leakage/seepage cases usually receive compensation under five headings:

1. Cost of repair: to repair the damage to the Plaintiff's premises which include the replacement of building parts, as per Shum Chi Yung and Another v Lam Chung Kwong and Another [2006], Lai Yuen Wah and Another v Chan Sai and Another [2006];
2. Damages: damages to any parts of the premises: e.g. damage to floors and wall tiles and other parts of premises (e.g. Tai Wai Lam v Ho Ka Tung and Another [2005], Wong Huen Min v Wong-Kong Chong-Kam-Sau Tong Clansman Association Ltd and Another [2007], Chan Yip Cheung v Fong Chow Wo [2008]);
3. Inconvenience: apart from inconvenience which is caused by the negative externality, such as water leaks to the immediate floor beneath, also refer to the time spent by the plaintiff due to visiting and cleaning their units, e.g. Chan Yip Cheung v Fong Chow Wo [2008];

Table 2.5 Keywords used in searching for relevant court cases in Hong Kong Law Report

Types of externality	Keyword use in Hong Kong Law Report
Air	Smell (151)
	Air (1972)
	Heat (266)
	Odour (34)
Noise	Noise (560)
Water	Water leakage (230)
	Water seepage (126)

4. Professional/expert fees: fees for preparing reports (e.g. Hung Tung Shing and Another [2002], Larbons Ltd v Kuo You Weaving Factory Ltd [2007]) and tests carried out by the Plaintiff's expert, (e.g. Costantino Gonnella v Dart Co Ltd [2008]);
5. Loss of rental: property has been reduced in value as a result of the water leakage problem and expenses for alternative accommodation (Lai Yuen Wah and Another v Chan Sai and Another [2006]);
6. Other possible headings include medical expenses, costs of finding alternative accommodation, etc.

In the case of noise pollution, however, it is seldom to see a clear breakdown. The majority of cases in Hong Kong Law Reports only show the total amount that the defendants need to pay.

2.5 Data

Data from First Instance Court cases were mainly collected from Hong Kong Law Reports. These keep records of court decisions from as early as 1905. By using the keyword search "water leakage", "noise" and "air", a large number of court cases appear. Numbers in brackets indicates the number of cases existing in the database. After the keyword search, each of the files was read to find out if the externality(ies) (either air, noise or water pollution) occurring in one place affect the residents in residential units, ultimately leading to litigation (Table 2.5).

2.6 Results

2.6.1 Water Seepage/Leakage

Although Hong Kong has a long history of litigation, Hong Kong Law Reports recorded the first water leakage case in 1994. From 1996 to 2000, there were only four cases. The figure then increased 5-fold to 20 in the period 2001–2005. From 2006 to 2010, there were 40 cases—10 times that from 1996 to 2000. The results

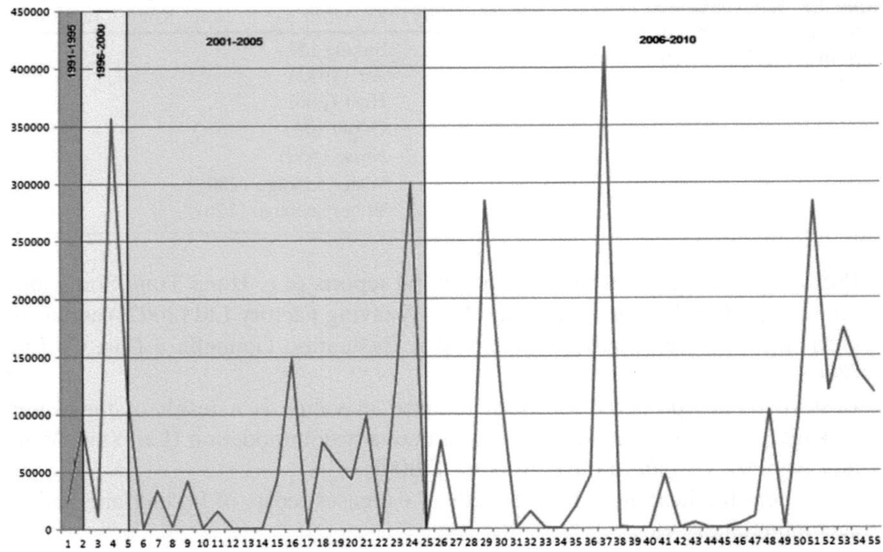

Fig. 2.3 Value of compensation (deflated by GDP deflator, year 2007 = 100) for water seepage/leakage court cases (start from 1994 as number 1). *Note* Plaintiffs of number 25 and 45 won the case but the amount to be compensated had not been mentioned in the report

not only indicate that the number of compensation court cases in residential buildings rose significantly, amount of compensation also climbed significantly. The total amount of compensation from 2001 to 2005 was twice that of 1996–2000, while the figure for 2006–2010 was ten-fold that of 2001–2005.

The court cases illustrate different methods which could be used to deal with negative environmental externality. Apart from requesting compensation from households which caused water seepage, the defendant in case numbers 22, 31 and 44 were ordered to perform the repairs and stop the source of pollution. The defendant in case 40 was restrained from installing or erecting any air-conditioners, pipes or other fittings at the external wall of the Building which was not provided under the Deed of Mutual Covenant (Fig. 2.3, Table 2.6).

2.6.2 Noise Pollution

Number of noise pollution court case was far less than that of water seepage. There were 16 cases only. The first court case appeared in 1998. In 1996–2000, there were 4 cases and all the plaintiff win. In 2001–2005, 2 out of 3 cases' plaintiffs fail to receive any compensation. Although there were 7 court cases in 2006–2010, only 1 plaintiff out of 7 cases won and received his compensation. In Jack Gordon Leslie Smith and Another v Tam Wing Wah and Anotherthe, the Tams installed

Table 2.6 Amount of compensation for water leakage (1991–2010)

Year	Repair fee	Damages	Medical expenses	Damages for personal damages	Inconvenience	Professional fees	Loss in rental	Removal costs	Alternative accommodation	Management fee	Total
1991–1995 (1 case, 0 plaintiff lost the cases)											
1994	1	23551	0	0	0	0	0	0	0	0	23551
1996–2000 (4 cases, 0 plaintiff lost the cases)											
Sum	481278	0	0	0	85615	4398	0	0	0	0	571291
Ave	120320	0	0	0	21404	1099	0	0	0	0	142823
SD	156428	0	0	0	33421	2199	0	0	0	0	
2001–2005 (20 cases, 4 plaintiffs lost the cases)											
Sum	238441	471435	2892	15897	48205	39115	31837	3385	0	248	991815
Ave	11922	23572	145	795	2410	1956	1592	169	0	12	49591
SD	22267	71592	647	3555	6038	4862	6022	757	0	56	
2006–2010[a] (40 cases, 5 plaintiffs lost the cases)											
Sum	950481	333272	1815	0	328788	138293	6438	0	35379	0	2078534
Ave	23762	8332	45	0	8220	3457	161	0	884	0	51963
SD	67666	38302	331	0	36249	16225	897	0	5266	0	

[a] *Note* Data in 2010 consists of January and February only

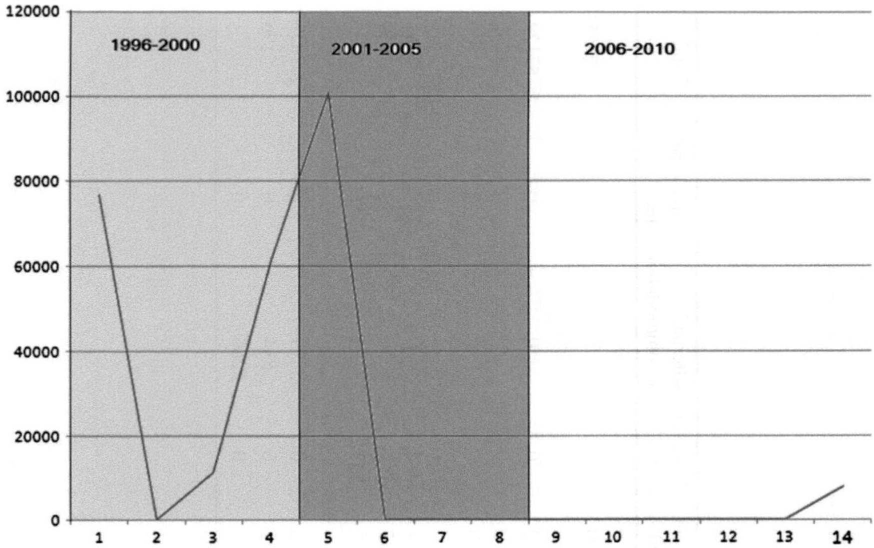

Fig. 2.4 Noise pollution compensation residential cases (start from the first case in 1998 as number 1, defendants of number 2 and 10 were ordered to stop producing noise, plaintiff of case number 9 received costs of proceedings only)

four loudspeakers in their garden and played amplified music. The judge considered that Smith had unreasonable requirements on quietness and therefore dismissed the case. Whist many of the noise complaints were neighborhood noise cases in residential areas, this might provide useful hint on why few cases successfully received compensation in court (Fig. 2.4).

2.6.3 Air Pollution

In the past, most of the flat owners relied on "bad air lowers value of residential units" to seek for reduction of Rate payable to the government, for example, Cheung Fat-Fan and Madam Fu Ah-kum and Commissioner of Rating and Valuation [1977], Lee Kan and Yip Hon-Ching and Commisionner of Valuation [1978]. There were also criminal case which arose under the air pollution ordinance: the contractor was responsible for a construction site where work had to be carried out in accordance with the Schedule, e.g. HKSAR v China State Construction Engineering (Hong Kong) Limited [2005]. Nevertheless, there was only one court case where the residential owner sued the air and noise pollutant producer. This failing precedent showed the difficulty in seeking air pollution compensation to internalize externality without help from the third party, i.e. government.

In Westlands Estates Limited and Egremont Estates Limited v Swilynn (HK) Limited [1985], the plaintiff contended that the heat and noise nuisance during the summer months adversely affected the salability of several residential units opposite to the installations. The plaintiff applied for assessing damages to be compensated with reference to "nuisance". Nevertheless, the application failed as there was no evidence as to the degree of heat and noise produced by the defendant's installations. Besides, it remained arguable that the heat emission was reasonable. The judge commented that the matter was not beyond argument. Therefore, the defendant must have unconditional leave to defend in case of nuisance.

2.7 Discussion and Conclusion

Hong Kong Law Report reviewed that there was substantially more successful cases which sought for compensation due to water seepage/leakage than noise and air pollution problem. The results agree with the author's hypothesis that the costs of identifying the source of pollutants are a lot lower in the water seepage and therefore more cases would be found in Hong Kong. As Hong Kong is a densely populated city, it is often difficult to locate the air pollutant defendant, e.g. who should be blamed for the poor air next to highway? How about pollutants arise from somewhere outside Hong Kong? Similarly, noise which affects the residents, such as quarreling in the next door may not occur every day. Nevertheless, evidence of damages can be found easily in water seepage cases. Transaction costs in searching for the defendant are lower than noise and air pollution problems.

Acknowledgments This chapter is a revised version of the paper "Li RYM (2012) The internalization of environmental externalities affecting dwellings: a review of court cases in Hong Kong. Economic Aff 32(2):81–87".

References

Anderson RI, Fok R, Zumpano LV, Elder HW (1998) Measuring the efficiency of residential real estate brokerage firms. J Real Estate Res 16:139–158

Baily MN (1993) Competition, regulation, and efficiency in service industries. Brookings Pap Econ Act 2:71–130

Baranzini A, Ramirez JV (2005) Paying for quietness: the impact of noise on geneva rents. Urban Stud 42:633–646

Calliess GP, Mertens J (2011) Transnational corporations, global competition policy, and the shortcomings of private international law. Indiana J Glob Leg Stud 18:843–872

Calvani T (1982) The mushrooming brunswick defense: injury to competition, not to plaintiff. Antitrust Law J 50:319–345

Centaline Property Agency (2013) Centamap. http://hk.centamap.com/gc/home.aspx. Accessed 30 Jan 2013

Chattopadhyay S (1999) Estimating the demand for air quality: new evidence based on the Chicago housing market. Land Econ 75:22–38
Chay KY, Greenstone M (2005) Does air quality matter? evidence from the housing market. J Polit Econ 113:376–424
Chockalingam S, Sornakumar (2011) Tools for improving safety performance of indian construction industry-AWH & SIT approach. Eur J Econ Financ Adm Sci 35:15–22
Coase RH (1960) The problem of social costs. J Law Econ 3:1–44
Cohen JP, Coughlin CC (2007) Spatial hedonic models of airport noise, proximity, and housing prices. J Reg Sci 48:859–878
Cohen JP, Coughlin CC (2009) Changing noise levels and housing prices near the Atlanta airport. Growth and Change 40:287–313
Connor JM (2004) Global antitrust prosecutions of modern international cartels. J Ind Compet Trade 4:239–267
Crocker TD, Anderson RJ (1971) Air pollution and residential property values. Urban Stud 8:171–180
Deyak TA, Smith VK (1974) Residential property values and air pollution: some new evidence. Q Rev Econ Bus 14:93–100
Environmental Protection Department (2011) Laws and regulation. http://www.epd.gov.hk/epd/english. Accessed 13 Feb 2011
Epp DJ, Al-Ani KS (1979) The effect of water quality on rural nonfarm residential property values. Am J Agric Econ 61:529–534
Gamble HB, Sauerlender OH, Langley CJ (1974) Adverse and beneficial effects of highways on residential property values. Transp Res Rec 583:36–44
Glofcheski R (2009) Tort law in Hong Kong. Sweet and Maxwell, Hong Kong
Gonzalez F, Leipnik M, Mazumder D (2013) How much are urban residents in Mexico willing to pay for cleaner air? Environ Dev Econ 18:354–379
Ham YJ, Maddison DJ, Elliott RJR (2013) The valuation of landfill disamenities in Birmingham. Ecol Econ 85:116–129
Henning JA, Ridker RG (1967) The determinants of residential property values with special reference to air pollution. Rev Econ Stat 49:246–257
Jauregui A, Hite D (2010) The impact of real estate agents on house prices near environmental disamenities. Hous Policy Debate 20:295–316
Jon PN (2004) Meta-analysis of airport noise and hedonic property values—problems and prospects. J Transp Econ Policy 38:1
Kirkwood JB, Lande RH (2008) The fundamental goal of antitrust: protecting consumers, not increasing efficiency. Notre Dame Law Rev 83:191–244
Kovacic WE (1996) The competiton policy entrepreneur and law reform in formerly communist and socialist countries. Am Univ Int Law Rev 11:437–474
Li RYM (2009) Private property rights, legal enforcement and economic prosperity: the fall of early civilized China and the Rise of United Kingdom in 18–19th Century. Asian Soc Sci 5:10–15
Li RYM (2013) Pricing the environmental externalities: a tale of Hong Kong and United Kingdom. In: 8th Annual Conference of The Asian Studies Association of Hong Kong. Hong Kong
Li RYM, Hung R (2013) Rostow's stages of growth model, "Urban Bias" and sustainable development in India. J Contemp Issues in Bus Res 2:170–178
Luttik J (2000) The value of trees, water and open space as reflected by house prices in the Netherlands. Landscape and Urban Plan 48:161–167
Manu PA, Ankrah A, Proverbs DG, Suresh S (2012) Investigating the multi-causal and complex nature of the accident causal influence of construction project features. Accid Anal Prev 48:126–133
McGehee JJ (2001) Developing interdisciplinary units: a strategy based on problem solving. Sch Sci Math 101:380–389
Meadowcroft J (2004) Externalities and the properrole of government. Econ Aff 24:77

Mendelsohn RD, Hellerstein M, Huguenin RU, Brazee R (1992) Measuring hazardous waste damages with panel models. J Environ Econ Manage 22:259–271
Morantz AD (2009) Has devolution injured American workers? state and federal enforcement of construction safety. J Law Econ Organ 25:183–210
Nahman A (2011) Pricing landfill externalities: emissions and disamenity costs in Cape Town, South Africa. Waste Manag 31:2046–2056
Navon R, Kolton O (2006) Model for automated monitoring of fall hazards in building construction. J Constr Eng Manage 132:733–740
Nelson AC, Genereux J, Genereux M (1992) Price effects of landfills on house values. Land Econ 68:359–365
Nelson JP (1978) Residential choice, hedonic prices, and the demand for urban air quality. J Urban Econ 5:357–369
Nelson JP (1982) Highway noise and property values: a survey of recent evidence. J Transp Econ Policy 16:117
Pennington G, Topham N, Ward MR (1990) Aircraft noise and residential property values adjacent to Manchester International Airport. J Transp Econ Policy 25:49–59
Ridker RG, Henning JA (1967) The determinants of residential property values with special reference to air pollution. Rev Econ Stat 49:246–257
Roberts GR (1996) The NCAA, antitrust, and consumer welfare. Tulane Law Rev 70:2631–2674
Takigawa T (2009) Competition law and policy of Japan. Antitrust Bull 54:435–515
Taylor SM, Breston BE, Hall FL (1982) The effect of road traffic noise on house prices. J Sound Vib 80:523–541
Thayer M, Albers H, Rahmatian M (1992) The benefits of reducing exposure to waste disposal sites: a hedonic housing value approach. J Real Estate Res 7:265–282
The National Archives (2012) The Construction (Health, Safety and Welfare) Regulations 1996. http://www.legislation.gov.uk/uksi/1996/1592/regulation/5/made. Accessed 25 July 2012
Theebe MAJ (2004) Planes, trains, automobiles: the impact of traffic noise on house prices. J Real Estate Financ Econ 28:209–234
Wadick P (2010) Safety culture among subcontractors in the domestic housing construction industry. Struct Surv 28:108–120
White L, Smith H, Currie C (2011) OR in developing countries: a review. Eur J Oper Res 208:1–11
Young CE (1984) Perceived water quality and the value of seasonal homes. Water Resour Bull 20:163–168

Chapter 3
The Institutional Analysis of Fittings in Residential Units

Abstract New institutional economists state that the different arrangements in informal and formal institutions affect the transaction costs and the institutional arrangements. Nanjing, Hong Kong and Boston represent three different cities immersed in 3 different cultures. The Chinese in Nanjing are immersed in Eastern culture. Hong Kong, a British colony for 150 years with Chinese as the majority group, is a unique city with a mixture of Western and Eastern culture. Boston is a city with a western culture. Apart from these cultural differences, these cities also have different economic, historical and legal backgrounds. How do formal (legal) and informal institutions (e.g., culture) affect the provisions of fittings by developers? No research has been conducted on this topic. Motivated by curiosity, this chapter aims to fill this gap in the research.

Keywords Institutional economics · Housing · Fittings

3.1 Introduction

I still remembered when I was still a PhD student, one of my PhD mates came from Bangladesh, he told me that the bed has to be placed in some special position in his hometown. I asked him why. He said "it is because of culture. I guess there are something similar in Hong Kong." Indeed, informal institutions affect our everyday lives. To certain extent, because we get to know when we are little, it is quite often that we consider culture as something which is nature and normal. Not until some foreigners talk with us, we then all of sudden noticed that this is not "in line with" the outside World. For example, the tie in sale of fittings with residential units are common in Hong Kong but not so in some areas such as China.

Apart from informal intuitions, regulations and enforcement affect the decisions made by us. For example, as a pedestrian, we feel save to walk pass the road in Hong Kong and the UK once the green light is on. Green light means all drivers in whatever directions have to stop. Yet, the same principle does not apply in places

R. Y. M. Li, *Law, Economics and Finance of the Real Estate Market*,
SpringerBriefs in Economics, DOI: 10.1007/978-3-642-54245-9_3,

around the World. For example, in Taiwan, China and Australia, the green light on the road only signifies that drivers in one direction have to stop but not all the directions. Their differences in behaviors of course, are due to the differences in regulations. In fact, economists recognized the impact of law on our society for a long time. In the book Wealth of Nation, Smith was aware of the impact of legal regulations on firm. Later, Marshall's research found that legislation in 19th century facilitated companies' capacity to obtain capital for investment. Legal system, therefore, is an important fuel in a company and provides a good environment for business entities (Li 2011a; Li and Li 2013a, b). Indeed, formal institutions like law are one of major factors which affect businessmen's decisions. Different arrangement in residential units sale (whether the fittings are tied in with the residential units) can be explained by formal (legal) and informal institutions (everything outside the regime of legal arrangements, such as culture, norms, economic system).

It is common to find an entire block of buildings with standardised fittings such as wall and floor tiles and kitchen and bathroom TVs provided by developers in Hong Kong. The term "one country (China), two systems" is one of the best descriptions for the provision of internal fittings. In Nanjing, 80 % of the residential developers provide empty flats with no more than the basic fittings such as windows, doors, and ironmongery. There are NO wall paintings, floor tiles, sanitary fittings, or kitchenwares. In Boston, apart from the standardised housing, it is not unusual to find a builder advertising a "Unique and open floor plan with high quality materials. Will tailor to your needs. Developer will work with you fully throughout the construction process to your satisfaction" (Toll Brothers 2008). Many builders, such as Altier Homes, Windswept Custom Homes, Designer Built Homes, etc., mention their ability and willingness to build customised homes (Fig. 3.1). Why there is such a large difference between these cities, from the empty standardised flats in China to well-equipped standardised flats in Hong Kong and from well-equipped standardised flats in Hong Kong to well-equipped customized flats in the US? How do informal and formal institutions affect the choices in the provision of fittings? This chapter begins with a brief description of the history of the three selected cities, followed by a literature review covering the three cities' cultures, economics and legal systems.

3.2 Background of Nanjing, Hong Kong and Boston

Among the many cities in the US and China, three cities have been chosen for this study: Nanjing, Boston and Hong Kong. These three cities are selected because of their special culture and historical background.

Fig. 3.1 Atlanta's Premier Home Builder's advertisement (author's photo)

3.2.1 Nanjing

Nanjing was the capital for 6 dynasties in China and became an important Chinese city during the first 1000 years of Chinese history because of its geographical location along the Yangzi River. In 3 A.D., Nanjing was designated for the first time as a capital. It has a long an important history in China. The famous Song dynasty lyricist Xin Qiji once exclaimed about the city, "I have come to mourn over the ancients…. the rises and falls of kingdoms fill my vision." The earliest Chinese historical accounts refer to the site in 496 B.C. as Yecheng, and it was established by Fuchai, the leader of the State of Wu. This city later became known as Yuecheng after the Wue lost a power struggle with the Yue. During medieval times, Nanjing served as the first of many capitals; the city was named Jianye in 3 A.D., which literally means "establishing the enterprise of founding a dynasty." Nanjing was also officially designated the capital of the Tang Dynasty; it was then known as Jiangkang. The Southern Tang kingdom and the powerless last emperor Li Yu termed Nanjing Jiangningfu, "The Administrative District of Jiangning," and made its capital there. Yuanzhang, who was the first emperor of the Ming Dynasty, overthrew the Yuan Dynasty and made Nanjing the capital again in 1368, calling her Yingtianfu (Honey 1995). Although there are 374 country-level cities, 15 sub-provincial cities and 283 prefecture-level cities, Nanjing was chosen for this study because of her special historical background.

3.2.2 Hong Kong

There are few cities similar to Hong Kong, which contains both Eastern and Western culture. In 1841, at the time of the cession of the island to the British Crown, the first proclamation made Captain Elliot the "Chief Superintendent of Trade and Her Majesty's Plenipotentiary in China" (Hsu 1992). Hong Kong was leased to the British by the Sino-British treaties signed between the Ching and the British Government in 1842, 1860, and 1898 (Postiglione 1991). The colonisation of the British marked a transformation in the structure of Chinese society in Hong Kong. Although there were only 90,000 people in Hong Kong in 1841, the floods of immigrants that rolled in first from the Taiping Rebellion (1851–1864), followed by the Chinese Revolution of 1911 and the political strife during 1941–1945 (Hsu 1992), led to rapid population growth in Hong Kong. One hundred years after the British leased Hong Kong, the city was returned to the control of mainland China.

3.2.3 Boston

Boston, located in Massachusetts, is the location of the famous "Boston Tea Party". Boston is one of the oldest cities in the US Archaeological remains reveal that the earliest settlers' activities can be dated back to 10,000 years ago. Similar to Hong Kong, Boston became a British colony in 1630 and independent after an important political victory and became independent in 1783 after these British colonies won independence (Secretary of the Commonwealth 2008).

3.3 Institutions and Contractual Arrangement

North (1990) defines institutions as the 'rules of the game in the society'. Organisations are 'players' in a game that is predefined by these rules (Lewins 2007). Specifically, both formal and informal institutional environments generate constraints that influence the behaviour of a firm.

3.3.1 Formal Institutions

Formal constraints include laws and regulations, which are drafted, implemented and enforced by authority. Law serves as social order, i.e. the relations between individuals (Li 2011a). The importance of formal institutions is highlighted in Coase (2008) "If we move from a regime of zero transaction costs to one of positive transaction costs, what becomes immediately clear is the crucial importance of the legal system in this new world…what are traded on the market are not, as is often supposed by economists, physical entities, but the rights to perform certain actions, and the rights which individuals possess are established by the legal system" (See the role of law in 3.5 for details).

3.3.2 Informal Institutions

On the other hand, informal constraints includes a society's culture and ideology (North 1981; Viet 2005). They regulate private and public affairs in modern societies and can hence be expected to exert an important influence on individuals' well-being (Bjørnskov et al. 2010). Informal institutions include:

1. Clientelism (the expression of political loyalty to providers of patronage);
2. Charisma (an authority relationship based on personal conviction and trust);
3. Collective self-defense (for instance, the development of shared norms of noninterference and sovereignty);
4. Pooling (horizontal exchanges within small groups of people) (Bratton 2007).

Informal institutions may emerge from repeated long term interactions (Farrell and Héritier 2003; Wu 2009) and can affect the distribution of resources, which in turn has an impact on the establishment of formal institutions (Viet 2005). Interested parties and the general public mainly impose their influences in the form of criticisms and ''bureaucratic bargaining'' to demonstrate their attitudes and requirements (He 2009). The role of informal rules has been underlined in numerous analyses of a wide range of phenomena, for example, networks, social values and norms in general, but also spontaneous cronyism, privatization, corruption, tunneling, labor hoarding, barter, arrears, tax evasion, informal economy (Chavance 2008).

The organisational cultures of firms are heavily influenced by culture and other aspects of the institutional environments in which they operate (Oliver 1997). The 1993 Nobel Prize winning economist North (1990) suggested that the main function of institutions is to reduce transaction costs in the economy. The choice of housing developers regarding the fittings of provisions is one example that realises North's view. The changes in knowledge sharing method from face to face to simple information technology tool like Web 1.0 (view only website) and from Web 1.0 to Web 2.0 (websites viewers can view, write and edit, e.g. Facebook, blog, Youtube) is another example (Li and Poon 2009, 2011; Li 2010; Li and Ah Pak 2010 and 2013).

Out of the seas of bolts and nuts in culture, individualism/collectivism play one of the most important role in our society. Hofstede (1991) defines individualism and collectivism as follows: "individualism pertains to societies in which the ties between individuals are loose: everyone is expected to look after himself or herself and his or her immediate family. Collectivism is the opposite and pertains to societies in which people from birth onwards are integrated into strong, cohesive groups which throughout people's lifetime continue to protect them in exchange for loyalty."

The core element of individualism is that individuals are independent of one another. From this perspective, a number of plausible implications or consequences of individualism can be discerned. Individualism focus on individuals' rights above duties, a concern for oneself as well as immediate family, an emphasis on self-fulfillment and personal autonomy, and one's identity on his personal accomplishments. With regard to self-concept, individualism implies that:

1. Abstract traits (as opposed to situational and social descriptors) are central to self-definition;
2. Creating and maintaining a positive sense of self is a basic fundamental human endeavor;
3. Feeling good about oneself, personal success, and having many unique or distinctive personal attitudes and opinions are valued (Oyserman et al. 2002).

Second, with regard to well-being, individualism implies attainment of one's personal goals and an open emotional expression are important sources of life satisfaction and well-being. Third, individualism implies that judgment, causal inference and reasoning are generally oriented toward the person rather than the situation or social context as decontextualized self is assumed to be a stable and causal nexus (Oyserman et al. 2002).

With regard to the self, collectivism implies that:

1. Valued personal traits reflect the goals of collectivism, for example, maintaining harmonious relationships with close others and sacrifice for the common good.
2. Group membership is a central identity (Oyserman et al. 2002).

Second, with regard to emotional expression and well-being, collectivism implies that:

1. Restraint in open and direct expression of personal feelings, is valued as a means of ensuring in-group harmony;
2. Life satisfaction comes from successfully carrying out social obligations and roles and avoiding failures in these areas (Oyserman et al. 2002).

People have access to different cultural patterns, including individualism and collectivism, in places all over the world. However, people in individualism-dominated countries, for example, the US, tend to have individualistic characters. The idea of liberalism, freedom and the striving for individual rights can be found in the Massachusetts Constitution as early as the 18th century. This document reads "All men are born free and equal, and have certain natural, essential, and unalienable rights; among which may be reckoned the right of enjoying and defending their lives and liberties; that of acquiring, possessing, and protecting property; in fine, that of seeking and obtaining their safety and happiness." On the

Table 3.1 Individualism and collectivism domains (Oyserman et al. 2002)

Domain name	Description	Sample item
Collectivism		
Related	Considering close others an integral part of the self	To understand who I am, you must see me with members of my group
Belong	Wanting to belong to and enjoy being part of groups	To me, pleasure is spending time with others
Duty	The duties and sacrifices being a group member entails	I would help, within my means, if a relative were in financial difficulty
Harmony	Concern for group harmony and that groups get along	I make an effort to avoid disagreements with my group members
Advice	Turning to close others for decision help	Before making a decision, I always consult with others
Context	Self changes according to context or situation	How I behave depends on who I am with, where I am, or both
Hierarchy	Focus on hierarchy and status issues	I have respect for the authority figures with whom I interact
Group	A preference for group work	I would rather do a group paper or lab than do one alone
Individualism		
Independent	Freedom, self-sufficiency, and control over one's life	I tend to do my own thing, and others in my family do the same
Goals	Striving for one's own goals, desires, and achievements	I take great pride in accomplishing what no one else can accomplish
Compete	Personal competition and winning	It is important to me that I perform better than others on a task
Unique	Focus on one's unique, idiosyncratic qualities	I am unique—different from others in many respects
Private	Thoughts and actions private from others	I like my privacy
Self-know	Knowing oneself; having a strong identity	I know my weaknesses and strengths
Direct	Communicate clearly articulating one's wants and needs	I always state my opinions very clearly

contrary, individuals in collectivism-dominated cultures such as Chinese culture are more likely to have a collectivistic tendency that emphasises interdependency and sacrifice for others within the group (Hampton and Xiao 2007). Differences between individualism and collectivism are shown in Table 3.1.

One of the major problems by relying on informal institutions rests in asymmetric information (see the examples in Table 3.2) as "[i]nformation is random and miscellaneous. We are flooded by messages from the instant everywhere in excruciating profusion… The latest information on anything and everything is collected, diffused, received, stored, and retrieved before anyone can discover whether the facts have meaning" (Acharya et al. 2009). If the network is small, relying on informal institutions human relationship works well as buyers and sellers may know each other well. Nevertheless, it becomes a problem when our

Table 3.2 Examples of asymmetric information (Li 2011b)

Business activity	Asymmetric information example
Bank	A borrower knows more than bankers about his or her chance of default
Firm investment	Although some investors may have private information about a firm's fundamental value, conflicting interests of informed and uninformed traders not only increase a firm's value uncertainty but also make investors take a conservative view on the firm's future value
Higher education	The department head knows less about a perspective teaching staff's ability and attitude than the professors themselves
Agriculture	The tenant who rents a piece of land knows the soil quality better than the landlords do; he is in the best position to estimate the rent that he should pay
Stock	The managerial staff in a company knows more information about the company than other stockholders
Housing	Residential unit purchasers do not hold the same information as builders do

Table 3.3 Methods of lowering risk (Li 2011b)

Method to lower risk	Example
Brand name	Searching for better choices from formal and informal sources, using brand image/reputation or price as a quality guide, or shopping only in stores with a high-quality image
Risk sharing with others	Partnership, risk sharing contract, contracting and subcontracting
Selecting the less risky choice	Becoming an employee instead of an entrepreneur, purchasing insurance, choosing compromising brands
	Marketers have also successfully made use of tools such as money-back guarantees, warranties, and free trials to influence consumers' risk perception

market grows, new developers; for example, do not know buyers' taste. Estimation about their needs becomes difficult.

3.3.3 Informal and Formal Institutions

Informal institutions can reinforce, replace and undermine formal institutions. In conventional settings, the effectiveness and emergence of many formal institutions is endogenous to the informal institutions (Grzymala-Busse 2010). Risk-taking by firms can be explained by the use of informal institutions, for example, brand name, various risk sharing methods along with recourse to emerging formal institutions such as written contracts. Informal institutions remain important as mechanisms of risk management even when new formal institutions gradually develop (Steer and Sen 2010) (Table 3.3).

3.4 The Economic Systems of the Three Cities

Between 1958 and 1978, the Chinese economic system was a planned economy. Decision-making power rested with the ruling parties (Yu and Gu 2001). There was no housing market because the central government distributed dwellings to all citizens. Developers at that time were an asset of the government and only accomplished the goal of the ruling party. There was no competition between developers. Private developers and the residential market only emerged after the Open Door Policy in 1978. Therefore, the residential market in Nanjing is far from mature. In addition to the immaturity of the organisations for the developers, the legal system for housing transactions and the quality of workmanship is at the infancy stage compared to these same institutions in the UK or the US.

A laissez-faire policy was adopted in Hong Kong as early as the 19th century. Freedom of trade is one of the most important elements contributing to her economic success. Milton Friedman once commented that Hong Kong was one of the freest cities in the world. Similar to Hong Kong, Boston also has a market economy: developers and homebuyers are free to make their transactions.

The gross regional product per capita of Massachusetts, Hong Kong and Nanjing are US $56,592, US $42,123 and ¥50,944 (US $1 = ¥6.8) in 2007, respectively. There is no doubt that the home purchasers in Massachusetts, the richest city among the three, demand a higher quality dwelling than the residents of the poorer cities. Furthermore, because of the high average income in Boston, the opportunity costs of spending some time to look for a water closet, a bathtub, etc., is extremely high. It is less expensive for these residents to buy a dwelling from the developers that already has well-arranged fittings.

3.5 The Legal System of the Three Cities

The development of construction and real estate law in China has been affected by her historical and cultural background (Lam and Chen 2004). The Cultural Revolution in 1966–1976 witnessed the dismantling of most legal rules and regulations in China (Yu and Gu 2001). The legal system had to be rebuilt from scratch. Many of the courts are run without sufficient funding; some plaintiffs need to pay before they can sue the defendants. The final products of these suits are often unfair judgments. Most of the legal rules and regulations that had been drafted and implemented prior to the cultural revolution were destroyed during that period. Laws and regulations concerning the quality of dwellings first appear in the 1990s. These regulations, however, only provide a general quality requirement. There is no specific requirement for fittings as can be found in Hong Kong and Boston. If the contractors provide low-quality fittings, the developers can only sue the contractors based on breach of contract (Table 3.4).

Table 3.4 Laws governing the quality of fittings in Nanjing (Zhu 2003)

Urban real estate development operation management ordinance	
Chapter 3 Construction of a real estate development	Section 16: Real estate developer must comply with the quality, safety, and design requirement as stated in law
Chapter 4 Real estate management	Section 28: The real estate developer and the vendor should sign a contract concerning the dwelling transaction. It should specify the saleable and usable area, price, date of hand over, quality, property management and the consequence of breach of contract
	Section 31: When the developer hands over the well-furnished dwelling unit to the vendor, it should provide him/her with a certificate of quality
Construction company quality management regulations	
Chapter 4 Construction management	Section 21: Construction company must submit (1) construction inspection year plan, (2) certificate of construction company's qualifications

Besides, regulatory authorities are fragmented in nature in China. It is common to see the central government implements certain set of law in some areas before implementing these regulations into a larger areas. Whilst the original idea is good, such policy often leads to ambiguity in implementation. Furthermore, lack of detail legal drafting allows the officials to "make" their own set of interpretations to attain their own benefits. For example, laws concerning construction work quality are ambiguous. According to Large Scale construction project management guidance notes (2008) section 2(1), construction management in China has to be socialized, professionalized and scientific to conform with market's needs. Nevertheless, there are no clear definitions on what elements constitute "socialized", professionalized and scientific. Therefore, laws, regulations and rules only exist in black and white with limited practicality (Li 2011a).

Moreover, compliance with rules and regulations is not a very high priority in Chinese society. The famous thinker Laozi once commented that "the more restrictions and prohibitions there are in the world, the poorer the people will be …the more laws that are promulgated, the more thieves and bandits there will be." Another school of thinkers, Daoism, is of the view that conventional social obligations should be abolished. Although traditional legal school thinkers advocate that "punishments should be severe and definite so that people are scared of them" (Gunde 2002), the story of Sheung Yang—killed by a severe punishment that was drafted by himself—has often been quoted by other thinkers as representing the problem of strict rules and laws. After all, the legal system is used to consolidate the socialist economic base, enhancing socialist development (Tay and Leung 1995) and achieving the goals of the central government. In a nutshell, in Chinese society, the "human relationship" is more important than rules and regulations. Contractors often spend time building strong relationships with the official construction departments instead of seriously testing the infrastructure process. (Chan et al. 1999). In view of these cultural tendencies, the requirement of good workmanship as stated in Chapter 4 of the Construction Company Quality Management Regulations is not sufficient to ensure that a good quality of work is performed by the contractors. Even if people fully comply with the laws and regulations, the laws in Nanjing primarily focus on the quality of flats delivered by the developers to the homebuyers. The developers can only sue the contractors based on contract law. The provision of bare flats without any fittings is one way to manage their risks; otherwise, they would make contracts with these irresponsible contractors. After all, eliminating fittings relieves them of depending on the contractors to provide the appropriate quality.

Elliot declared the cession of the Hong Kong Island on 24 January 1841 and made the formal proclamation on 26 January in the same year. Common Law was introduced to Hong Kong by Captain Elliot in 1841: "pending Her Majesty's further pleasure our British subjects and foreigners residing in or resorting to the Island of Hong Kong shall enjoy full security and protection according to the principles and practice of British Law…Such of the laws of England as existed when the Colony obtained a local legislature, that is to say on 5th April 1843, shall be in force in the Colony, except so far as the said laws are inapplicable to the local circumstances of the Colony, or of its inhabitants, and except so far as they have been modified by laws passed by the said legislature…Law of England shall be in full force in the said colony of Hong Kong except where same shall be inapplicable to local circumstances of the said colony or of its inhabitants" (Hsu 1992). Although common law practice in Hong Kong has a rather short history, most of the regulations were copied with minor modifications from the UK, which has a very mature legal system compared to other jurisdictions. The Sale of Goods Ordinance implies that contractors need to provide reasonable workmanship and materials. If the contractors have provided poor services, the homebuyers can obtain compensation based on the Sale of Good Ordinance (legislation) as well as contract law (common law). In addition, Cap 123F specifies the minimum requirement for the provisions of fittings in the kitchen and bathroom. Developers must comply with the law's requirement. All of these factors account for why better furnished flats are provided in Hong Kong (Table 3.5).

In the United States, different states have their own laws. The rights and duties of the parties with respect to the contract are determined by state law. Unlike cases in China, however, any decisions made by a judge can be accessed by the general public through the Westlaw and Lexis services. To minimise any disputes concerning a contract, claims procedures are usually listed as "general conditions" in the construction contract. The architect is often given the power to decide disputes under the construction contract (Holland 2008). In addition, all construction of detached one- and two-family homes is regulated by the Board of Building Regulations and Standards. A contractor must be licensed as a Construction Supervisor prior to performing work on such homes (Commonwealth of Massachusetts 2008a). In a case where the contractors perform poorly, misrepresent a material fact by the applicant when obtaining a certificate of registration, or violate the building laws of the Commonwealth or of any political subdivision thereof, the developers or the prospective home owners can file complaints against the

Table 3.5 Legal regulations on the quality of fittings in Hong Kong

Regulations	Details
Cap 26 sale of goods ordinance section 2(5)	Goods of any type should be of merchantable quality: (1) Fit for the purpose(s) for which commonly purchased (2) Standard appearance and finish (3) Free from defects (4) Safe (5) Durable
Cap 123F building (planning) regulations	(1) Dwelling units must be provided with kitchen unless exempted by the building authority (2) The internal surface of every kitchen shall be either rendered in cement mortar or covered with tiles (3) Every kitchen should be provided with a sink and fittings for water supply and properly constructed cooking slab or fireplace (4) A room-sealed gas water heater must be provided in every bathroom in a building (5) If a room-sealed gas water heater is installed in any place other than the bathroom, appropriate provision must be made for the installation of such room-sealed gas water heater (6) No gate, window, door or shutter opening shall be placed at a height of less than 2.5 m above the ground level

Table 3.6 Massachusetts state building code (Commonwealth of Massachusetts 2008b)

Building code	Details
780 CMR 6501 clothes dryers exhaust	6501.1 General exhaust system. Dryer exhaust systems shall be independent of all other systems, shall convey the moisture to the outdoors and shall terminate on the outside of the building
780 CMR 6502 range hoods	6502.1 General range hoods shall discharge to the outdoors through a single wall duct. The duct serving the hood shall have a smooth interior surface, shall be air tight and shall be equipped with a back draft damper. Ducts serving range hoods shall not terminate in an attic or crawl space or areas inside the building

(continued)

contractors with the Board of Building Regulations and Standards under Massachusetts General Laws chapter 143. Although the submission of a complaint will not automatically result in a hearing against the contractor or any monetary award, the complaint may result in disciplinary action against the contractor's registration or license (Board of Building Regulations and Standards 2009). In addition, any prospective homeowner can check with the local clerk of court to see if there are

Table 3.6 (continued)

Building code	Details
780 CMR 6506 mechanical ventilation	6506.1 General. Where toilet rooms and bathrooms are mechanically ventilated, the ventilation equipment shall be installed in accordance with 780 CMR 6506
Minimum required exhaust rates for one- and two-family dwellings; area to be ventilated; ventilation rates	780 CMR 6506 Mechanical ventilation Kitchen 100 cfm intermittent or 25 cfm continuous Bathrooms—Toilet rooms mechanical exhaust capacity of 50 cfm intermittent or 20 cfm continuous
780 CMR 6601 Duct construction	6601.1.1 Above-ground Duct Systems Above-ground duct systems must conform to the following: 1. Equipment connected to duct systems shall be designed to limit discharge air temperature to a maximum of 250 °F (121 °C) 2. Factory-made air ducts shall be constructed of Class 0 or Class 1 materials as designated in 780 CMR Table 6601.1.1(1) 3. Fibrous duct construction shall conform to the SMACNA "Fibrous Glass Duct Construction Standards" or NAIMA "Fibrous Glass Duct Construction Standards" 4. Minimum thicknesses of metal duct material shall be as listed in Table 6601.1.1(2). Galvanised steel shall conform to ASTM A 525
780 CMR 8302 Building structure protection	8302.2 Penetrations of Fire-resistance-rated Assemblies. Electrical penetrations through fire-resistance-rated walls, floors, partitions or ceilings should be protected by approved methods to maintain the fire-resistance rating of the element penetrated
780 CMR 8.00 Interior finishes	803.4.4 Materials. An interior wall or ceiling finish that is not more than 6.4 mm thick must be applied directly against a non-combustible backing 804.3 Testing and Identification. Floor covering materials shall be tested by an approved agency in accordance with NFPA 253

any civil judgments or lawsuits pending against the contractor over, for example, poor workmanship (The American Bar Association 2008). In Boston, the channel for complaints regarding a new home is not limited to litigation; homeowner associations have gained in popularity. Since the 1980s, membership in a homeowner association has become a mandatory condition of ownership in some communities. According to the Community Association Institute because the early 1990s, approximately 80 % of newly constructed dwellings are governed by a homeowner association (Real Estate.Com 2007) (Table 3.6).

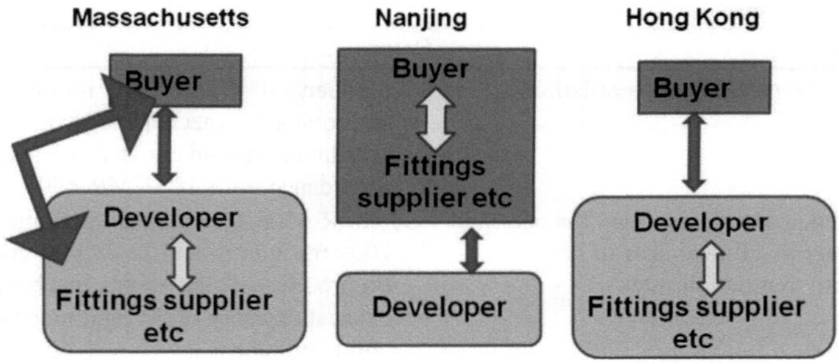

Fig. 3.2 Institutional arrangement in Boston, Nanjing and Hong Kong

Table 3.7 Differences between the three cities

Informal institutions/fittings in residential units	China (Nanjing)	Hong Kong	US (Massachusetts)
History	Capital of six dynasties in China	A Chinese city ruled by the UK for over 100 years	One of the oldest cities in US
Economy	Planned economy until 1979, mixed economy afterward	Market economy	Market economy
Individualism/collectivism	Collectivism	Collectivism	Individualism
Legalism	Weak	Strong	Strong
Fittings			
Bedroom doors	No	Yes	Yes
Kitchen			
Hood	No	Yes	Yes
Wall and floor tiles	No	Yes	Yes
Cupboard	No	Yes	Yes
Bathroom			
Wash basin	No	Yes	Yes
Water closet	No	Yes	Yes
Electrical boxes with covering?	No	Yes	Yes
Freedom for homebuyers to request a unique style for their individual dwellings?	No	No	Yes

3.6 Discussion

Figure 3.2 illustrates the differences in the contractual arrangements in the three cities and Table 3.7 summarises the major differences. The developers in Boston and Hong Kong provide all of the basic fittings in the dwellings to the buyers. The developers in these cities have contracts with the washroom and kitchen fittings suppliers, painters and floor tiles suppliers. The builders in Nanjing only provide the bare flats with nothing else. Homebuyers must make separate contracts with these fittings suppliers. In addition, the homebuilders in Massachusetts usually provide a choice to the prospective buyers in terms of the fittings (as indicated by the large arrowhead), which makes Boston unique among the three cities.

The developers in Boston specify that their services include providing a unique dwelling. Under the influence of liberalism and individualism, the cost of identifying the buyers' requirements for internal fittings became so high that the builders instead provide the buyers with the freedom to choose their fittings. In Hong Kong and China, where collectivism prevails, the buyers are more willing to accept the fittings provided by each dwelling within the residential development; the uniqueness of the dwelling is not the vendor's major concern. The costs of predicting the buyer's needs and demands are lower.

It is beyond all doubt that the pre-sale system for builders is an important source of financing for developers, whose projects require large sums of money and have a long project cycle. In recent years, however, complaints caused by the pre-sales of housing are increasing in China due to China's immature market economy and poor legal system. A heated debate has arisen about whether the housing pre-sale system should be abolished, with people holding both positive and negative views (Ding et al. 2007). While the findings indicate that slanted versus flat roof, sprinkler systems, garden baths, separate shower stalls, double ovens and gated communities positively affect the selling price (Sirmans et al. 2005), the developers in China only provide the most basic fittings primarily because of the high costs of enforcing the contract. These difficulties occur in China not only because of her immature legal system but also because the traditional ranking of law is low. People place a higher rank on human relationships than on the law, making it difficult for the developers to predict the quality of workmanship or the materials provided by the contractors.

Acknowledgments This chapter was a revised version of a paper originally presented as Li, Rita Yi Man (2009) How do business environment affect the behavior of businessmen? A triangular study on developers in Nanjing, Hong Kong and Boston, 3rd International Online Conference on Business & Management, 27–28th May 2009, E-Proceeding, a paper published in Li, Rita Yi Man (2010) A study on the impact of culture, economic, history and legal systems which affect the provisions of fittings by residential developers in Boston, Hong Kong and Nanjing, International Journal of Global Business and Management Research, Vol. 1, No. 3/4, pp. 131–141; and a book chapter published in Li, Rita Yi Man (2011) Everyday life application of Neo-institutional Economics Lambert Academic Publishing, Saarbrucken, Germany.

References

Acharya V, Philippon T, Richardson M, Roubini N (2009) The financial crisis of 2007–2009: causes and remedies. Financ Markets Inst Instrum 18:89–137

Bjørnskov C, Dreher A, Fischer JAV (2010) Formal institutions and subjective well-being: revisiting the cross-country evidence. Eur J Polit Econ 26:419–430

Board of Building Regulations and Standards (2009). Home Improvement Contractor Registration/Construction Supervisor License Complaint Application Form. http://www.mass.gov/Eeops/docs/dps/appl/appl_csl-hic_complaint.pdf. Accessed 30th April 2009

Bratton M (2007) The democracy barometers formal versus informal institutions in Africa. J Democracy 18:96–110

Chan WKL, Wong FKW, Scott D (1999) Managing construction projects in China—the transitional period in the millennium. Int J Proj Manage 17:257–263

Chavance B (2008) Formal and informal institutional change: the experience of postsocialist transformation. Eur J Comp Econ 5:57–71

Coase RH (2008) The institutional structure of production. In: Ménard C, Shirley MM (eds) Handbook of new institutional economics. Springer, Chicago

Commonwealth of Massachusetts (2008a) 7th edition one and two family dwellings. http://www.mass.gov/?pageID=eopsterminal&L=4&L0=Home&L1=Consumer+Protection+%26+Business+Licensing&L2=License+Type+by+Business+Area&L3=Home+Improvement+Contractor&sid=Eeops&b=terminalcontent&f=dps_780cmr&csid=Eeops. Accessed 30th March 2009

Commonwealth of Massachusetts (2008b) Massachusetts State building code. http://www.mass.gov/?pageID=eopsterminal&L=4&L0=Home&L1=Consumer+Protection+%26+Business+Licensing&L2=License+Type+by+Business+Area&L3=Home+Improvement+Contractor&sid=Eeops&b=terminalcontent&f=dps_780cmr&csid=Eeops. Accessed 20th March 2009

Ding LY, Chen XH, Sun J (2007) Research on optimal model of risk sharing about housing pre-sale system in China. In: 14th international conference on management science and engineering, Harbin

Farrell H, Héritier A (2003) Formal and informal institutions under codecision: continuous constitution-building in Europe. Gov Int J Policy Adm Inst 16:577–600

Grzymala-Busse A (2010) The best laid plans: the impact of informal rules on formal institutions in transitional regimes. Stud Comp Int Dev 45:311–333

Gunde R (2002) Culture and customs of China. Greenwood Press, London

Hampton NZ, Xiao F (2007) Attitudes toward people with developmental disabilities in Chinese and American students: the role of cultural values, contact, and knowledges. J Rehabil 73:23–32

He N (2009) Great influence of the economic factors to innovative technology utilization: international experiences for China telephony. Asian Soc Sci 5:109–113

Hofstede G (1991) Cultures and organizations: software of the mind, McGraw-Hill, London

Holland RT (2008) "True" breaches of contract: judicial review and the finality of decisions of an awarding authority on claims of a contractor on public construction projects in Massachusetts. Mass Law Rev 91:127–137

Honey DB (1995) Before dragons coiled and tigers crouched: early Nanjing in history and poetry. J Am Orient Soc 115:15–25

Hsu B (1992) The common law in Chinese context. Hong Kong University Press, Hong Kong

Lam YT, Chen ZG (2004) The development of the construction legal system in China. Constr Manage Econ 22:347–356

Lewins R (2007) Acknowledging the informal institutional setting of natural resource management: consequences for policy-makers and practitioners. Prog Dev Stud 7:201–215

Li RYM (2010) Knowledge sharing by Web 2.0 in real estate and construction discipline. In: Anandarajan M, Anandarajan A (eds) E-research collaboration: frameworks, tools and techniques. Springer, Heidelberg, pp 289–301

Li RYM (2011a) Everyday life application of neo-institutional economics. Lambert Academic Publishing, Saarbrucken

Li RYM (2011b) Imperfect information and entrepreneurs' choice on provision of house fittings. Lex Et Sci Econ Ser 18:269–276

Li RYM, Ah Pak DH (2010) Resistance and motivation to share sustainable development knowledge by Web 2.0. J Inf Knowl Manage 9:251–262

Li RYM, Li YL (2013a) The relationship between law and economic growth: a paradox in China. Asian Soc Sci 9:19–30
Li RYM, Li YL (2013b) The role of competition law: an Asian perspective. Asian Soc Sci 9:47–53
Li RYM, Poon SW (2009) Future motivation in construction safety knowledge sharing by means of information technology in Hong Kong. J Appl Econ Sci 4:457–472
Li RYM, Poon SW (2011) Using Web 2.0 to share the knowledge of construction safety as a public good in nature among researchers: the fable of economic animals. Econ Aff 31:73–79
Li RYM, Poon SW (2013) Construction safety. Springer, Berlin
North DC (1981) Structure and change in economic history. Norton, New York
North DC (1990) Institutions, institutional change and economic performance. Cambridge University Press, Cambridge
Oliver C (1997) Sustainable competitive advantage: combining institutional and resource-based views. Strateg Manage J 18:697–713
Oyserman D, Coon HM, Kemmelmeier M (2002) Rethinking individualism and collectivism: evaluation of theoretical assumptions and meta-analyses. Psychol Bull 128:3–72
Postiglione GA (1991) From capitalism to socialism? Hong Kong education within a transitional society. Comp Educ Rev 35:627–649
Real Estate.Com (2007) Homeowners associations: what you need to know before buying. http://www.realestate.com/tipsandtools/Homeowners-Associations/Homeowners-Associations-What-You-Need-to-Know-Before-Buying.aspx. Accessed 30th March 2009
Secretary of the Commonwealth (2008) Massachusetts facts. http://www.sec.state.ma.us/cis/cismaf/mafidx.htm
Sirmans GS, Macpherson DA, Zietz EN (2005) The composition of hedonic pricing models. J Real Estate Lit 13:3–43
Steer L, Sen K (2010) Formal and informal institutions in a transition economy: the case of Vietnam. World Dev 38:1603–1615
Tay AES, Leung CSC (1995) Greater China law, society and trade. The Law Book Company Limited, Victoria
The American Bar Association (2008) ABA guide to home ownership. http://www.abanet.org/publiced/practical/books/home_ownership/home.html. Accessed 30th March 2009
Toll Brothers (2008) Regency at Assabet Ridge. http://www.tollbrothers.com/communities/8846/lifestyle_brochure/lifestyle_guide.pdf. Accessed 5th May 2008
Viet NQ (2005) Do informal institutions matter?—confucian values on the transition to the rule of law in Vietnam. http://64.233.179.104/scholar?hl=zh-TW&lr=&q=cache:RppdHbFX_PkJ:aslea.org/paper/viet.doc+%22formal+and+informal+institution%22. Accessed 4th May 2008
Wu Y (2009) New institutionalism politics: integration of old institutionalism and other methodologies. Asian Soc Sci 5:105–108
Yu G, Gu M (2001) Laws affecting business transactions in the PRC. Kluwer Law International, Hague
Zhu M (2003) Construction project contract dispute. China Legal Publisher, Beijing

Chapter 4
Asymmetric Information and Residential Entrepreneurs' Choice on Provision of House Fittings

Abstract Running a real estate business is risky; it requires heavy capital investment in land, professional training and recruitment. Nevertheless, this huge expenditure does not guarantee a great return, and it is possible to suffer a substantial loss if the entrepreneur makes a wrong decision. Provision of home fittings is one of the risks that the housing entrepreneur faces. Some buyers dislike the fittings and thus decide not to purchase the home. In Hong Kong, land supply is scarce, but demand is huge (7 million people live in a small city with a hilly landscape). Land price occupies a relatively large proportion of the costs in dwelling production. Provision of a towel ring, washing basin, water closet, and other fittings only uses a small proportion of the total costs of construction. Besides, many developers have run their business for years and accumulated sufficient knowledge on buyers' taste. Nevertheless, in mainland China, especially in areas of low land costs, costs of fittings have become relatively high. The risk of supplying fittings that prospective owners dislike is higher. Many entrepreneurs do not wish to take the risk. This chapter aims at reviewing the asymmetric information and risks that housing entrepreneurs face in mainland China and analysing entrepreneurs' decision in response to this risk.

Keywords Imperfect Information · Entrepreneurs · Residential fittings · Housing

4.1 Introduction

Austrian economists postulate that no individual is homogeneous. Individuals act according to their experiences and knowledge. Hence, each of us foresees and predicts the future in different ways (Mingpao 2011). It is also assumed that people are endowed with different levels of innate talent; the more talented group become entrepreneurs and hire the less talented in equilibrium (Dearing et al. 2011). The when and where questions in entrepreneurs' business ventures are mainly determined by the social context, organisational norms, culture, history and power

R. Y. M. Li, *Law, Economics and Finance of the Real Estate Market*,
SpringerBriefs in Economics, DOI: 10.1007/978-3-642-54245-9_4,

considerations (Tan et al. 2010). Entrepreneurs in our society combine means of production, and their acts are crucial to economic development (Beck and Levine 2005). Entrepreneurs also deal with the "who" question. They create and organise new companies and hire workers with human capital. They also encourage workers to invest in their own education so that they can move into the modern production sector. Had entrepreneurs not existed, these educated workers might have had to take jobs that make inadequate use of their skills. They may not have been able to earn a high salary. The literature also reviews the importance of entrepreneurs in individuals' learning (Beck and Levine 2005), "whenever the economy takes a nosedive, it is typical for people to begin to dance with their "inner entrepreneur" and brainstorm ideas for launching their dream business" (Frey 2012).

Entrepreneurs also play a major role in profit making (Fugar and Agyakwah-Baah 2010) and assuming a large part of firms' risk (National Bureau of Statistics of China 2010; Li 2012). Theorists of entrepreneurship view entrepreneurs as individuals who bear residual uncertainty in running a business. Entrepreneurs must accept uncertainty in career security, family relations and psychic and financial well-being (Beck and Levine 2005). Starting from the moment an entrepreneur realises that their ideas possess market potential, they face the challenge of venture finance. Though some firms' business and financial strategies are laid out and agreed between the entrepreneur and interim investors, others depend on the entrepreneur only in seeking financial and strategic advice. This may increase entrepreneurs' momentum to raise any additional funds beyond their personal means, possibly from angel investors (Karkoulian et al. 2008). Concerning the supply of entrepreneurs in our market, some concur that the supply constitutes a key bottleneck to development and is inelastic in nature. Others hold the view that productive entrepreneurs can be summoned relatively quickly if the rules and institutions they determine are conducive to such activity because supply is always latent in the population (Dearing et al. 2011). Similar to any other type of entrepreneur, housing entrepreneurs combine the factors of production, and they have to make decisions on what, how and for whom to produce. They also have to accept the financial risks, e.g., the global financial crisis led to a drop in sales of newly built residential units.

4.2 Information, Imperfect Information and Asymmetric Information

Traditional thinking concurs that uncertainty creates the need for information processing. By way of proper problem formulation, information helps executives to create and select the appropriate course of action. Information also helps to stimulate creativity, monitor performance, determine environmental trends, generate scenarios and control activities. Furthermore, information is the major source of fuel in planning and strategizing. After all, executives simply cannot function without information (Tan et al. 2010). Although "information" is an important subject in many disciplines, it does not give rise to any economic interest by itself (Zou and Zhang 2009). In a world of positive transaction costs, imperfect information exists, and information has to be transmitted from one who knows it well to a receiver. Nevertheless, information sometimes backs up by information holders who fail to transmit it to individuals who wish to receive it (Pendharkar et al. 2008). Therefore, it is suggested that asymmetric information exists between sellers and purchasers (Tutzauer et al. 2006). Information asymmetry indicates that market participants possess unequal share of information (Naser and Moutinho 1997). The associated unobserved variables under asymmetric information may affect the cost and benefit (Zou and Zhang 2009), e.g., investors can reap more profit by acquiring rates of return information (Beavers et al. 2009); however, it may also cause home investors to suffer losses.

4.3 Risk-Averse Human Behaviour

Risk has been identified as the potential for negative consequences of an activity, a combination of exposure and hazard as well as the possibility of injury, damage or loss. And risk taking is one of the major attributes which is applicable to the individuals (Barry 1993). Recent literature focuses on the two-edged nature of risk, such as challenge and threat, and the probability that something will happen that will affect the original objectives of an act (Goh 2001). The risk attitude of an individual affects his behaviour and plays an important role in his decision making (Garrett and Teizer 2009; Hussein et al. 2010). For example, a retailer under demand uncertainty changes its pricing, purchasing, and service investment behaviour (Hussein et al. 2010). This premise lays important ground for many business activities (Arrow 1971), such as hedge funds, derivative sales, and agency contracts. Risk can be managed by easing and control, quantification and identification, catastrophe planning and financing (Goh 2001).

In general, individuals who choose not to act on an actuarially fair activity are classified as risk averse (Arrow 1971). Are people risk seeking or risk averse? Economists have shown that individuals tend to be risk averse ever since the era of Bernoulli (Li and Poon 2011) and security is mostly superstition in men's circle (Hagcvik 1999). In construction industry, risk averse culture tend to encourage flexible style of communication for different projects (Tran and Skitmore 2002). Though risk attitudes can also be explained by utility curvature, risk aversion holds if and only if the utility function has a concave shape, implying the basic assumption of diminishing marginal utility. Nevertheless, some previous research falsifies expected utility systematically as a descriptive theory of individual decision making, and extensive experiments have shown that risk aversion is more than the psychophysics of money. Furthermore, "this descriptive inadequacy has become the major inspiration for alternative theories development on individual decision making under risk" (Imriyas et al. 2008). Under the conjecture of risk averse, individuals try to lower the risks as long as the costs of doing are lower than the benefit (Li and Chau 2010). Risk-averse home purchasers, for example, prefer the option of "tried and true" (Logan and Moseley 2002). To minimise perceived risk, consumers may rely on various risk-reduction methods, e.g., reliance on brand names, sharing risk with others and selecting a less risky choice (Li 2010). The implementation of stringent technical requirements is attributed to people's risk-averse behavior (Mohan et al. 2013). They may also seek compensation for engaging in risky activities. Incentives to undertake risky projects that add value to the firm, such as salary and cash bonus, therefore emerge in our working environment (Matthews and Matthews 2010).

The degree to which people are risk averse, however, is not constant. Research has shown that people who are facing income uncertainty or constrained liquidity are relatively more risk-averse (Garrett and Teizer 2009). On the contrary Halek and Eisenhauer (2001) postulate that rich people are more risk averse. Similarly, many auction theorists view the principal as considerably more risk averse than its trading partners. For instance, a privatisation agency might be more risk averse than the bidders in a transitional economy (Rasoulinezhad 2011). The Friedman–Savage utility model recognizes that while most people tend to be risk-averse, there are individuals who prefer to take risks over certain income ranges (Basham and Luik 2011). People's attitudes towards risks are not stagnant. They become more risk averse as values fall (Cochrane 2011). Different nations display different attitude towards risks. For example, Chinese are risk averse and they only invest in projects that are believed to be profitable (Kjøllesdal and Welle-Strand 2010). In construction industry, they also prefer a stable project environment (Zou et al. 2009). In fact, many firms are risk averse and their attitude change from time to time. For instance, developers become extremely short-term-oriented and risk-averse as uncertainty increases (Li 2009b). Some companies hold more cash solely because their risk aversion on the part of management is above average in the aftermath of bankruptcies in previous years (Hussein et al. 2010). Others may not be willing to bid for contract to avoid risks (Abdi et al. 2013). Whalley (2011) models the investment choices of a risk-averse entrepreneur in an R&D project. Risk aversion is more likely to be an important factor in investors' decision making in smaller, privately owned firms than in large public corporations. The model is particularly relevant to, for e.g., research-based start-up firms.

4.4 Housing Entrepreneurs' Decisions on Provision of Fittings

In many places, including Hong Kong, housing entrepreneurs provide elaborate wall treatments, window frames, cupboards, floor tiles and electrical fittings. In some cases, developers also provide heated floors and wine storage. There is, however, a completely different norm in mainland China. For instance, the majority of

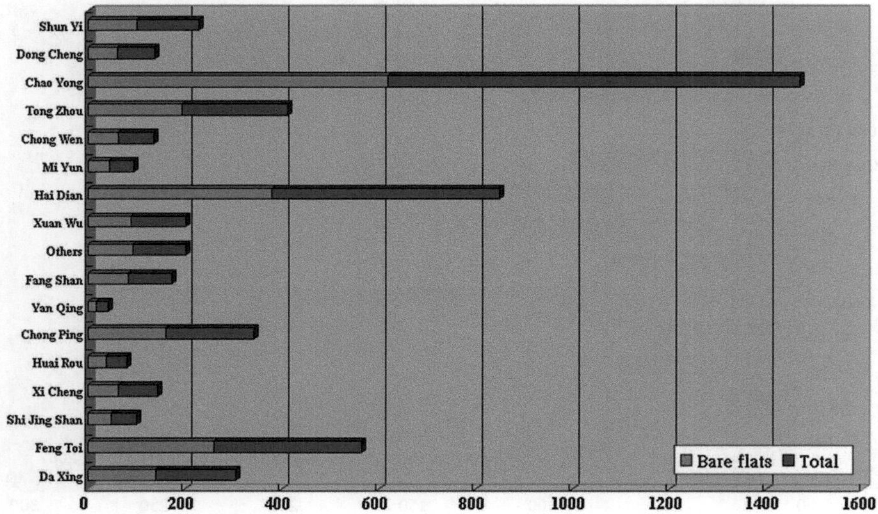

Fig. 4.1 Percentage of bare flats in Beijing from 1997 to 2008 (Li 2009a)

developers in Beijing and Nanjing sell roughcast flats to home purchasers. There are no towel rings, cupboards or basic bathroom fittings (Li 2009a). Among all first-hand residential units sold in Beijing districts, more than 70 % of them were bare units. Similarly, 90 % of the residential developments available for occupation in Nanjing were bare units. This finding simply implies that entrepreneurs in Beijing and Nanjing do not spend a penny on house fittings (see the Figs 4.1 and 4.2).

What is the major reason behind this finding? China is a newly emerging real estate market. There were no private companies prior to 1978 due to the planned economy. Many entrepreneurs are thus newcomers in the industry. They are not experienced sellers with plenty of information for predicting buyers' tastes in house fittings. In sharp contrast, repeated sales activities in other places, such as Hong Kong, Boston, and Australia enable local housing entrepreneurs in these locations to learn from their mistakes. No matter what, housing entrepreneurs are risk and loss averse. They all aim to maximise their profits and minimise the risk. To minimise risk, these entrepreneurs choose not to provide any fittings. Furthermore, traditional entrepreneurs relied upon many sources of external financing: debt, venture capital, private equity and public stock offerings. Investors who commit funds to business start-ups expect to receive back their invested sum of money along with a handsome return. Entrepreneurs must ask themselves if their goals are congruent with those of possible investors (Karkoulian et al. 2008). If housing entrepreneurs make an incorrect decision, such as putting undesirable fittings into their residential units, it will affect the other investors as well. Shareholders who invest in these companies will develop negative opinions about these entrepreneurs. Potential joint ventures may also become futile if the housing entrepreneurs have a history of incorrect decisions.

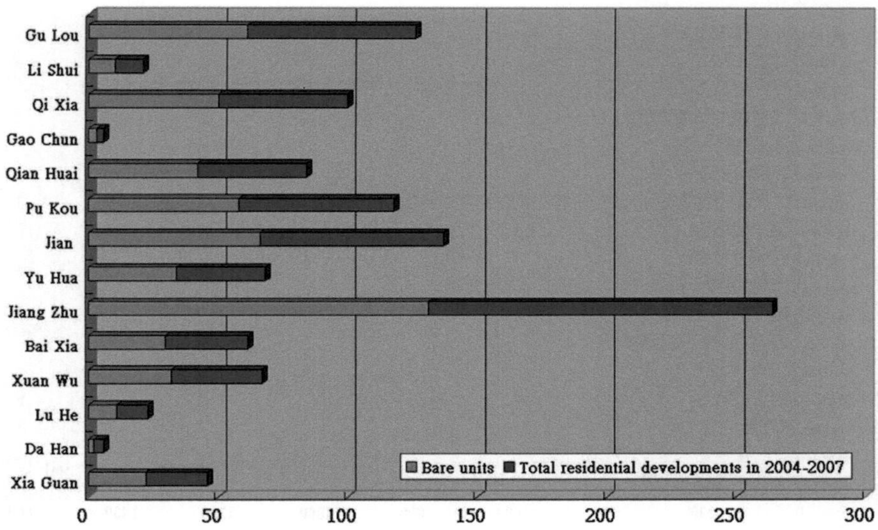

Fig. 4.2 Percentage of bare flats in Nanjing (Khan et al. 2011)

4.5 Conclusion

All entrepreneurs share one characteristic: they bear risk and earn some profit in return. Housing entrepreneurs are risk averse as well. They attempt to find ways to reduce their risk. Housing entrepreneurs in mainland China who provide bare units provide a vivid example of risk aversion.

Acknowledgment This chapter is a revised version of the paper "(Li, Rita Yi Man (2011) Imperfect Information and Entrepreneurs' Choice on Provision of House Fittings, Lex Et Sciential Economic Series, Vol. 18, No. 1, pp. 269–276". The author would like to thank the journal for agreeing to republish the paper.

References

Abdi A, Lind H, Birgisson B (2013) Payment mechanisms for winter road maintenance services. Australas J Constr Econ Building 13:18–31

Arrow KJ (1971) Essays in the theory of risk-bearing. North-Holland Publication Company, Amsterdam

Barry JM (1993) Vision, risk taking and personal commitment is there a connection? J Environ Health 56:29

Basham P, Luik J (2011) The social benefit of gambling. Econ Aff 31:9–13

Beavers JE, Moore JR, Schriver WR (2009) Steel erection fatalities in the construction industry. J Constr Eng Manag 135:227–234

Beck T, Levine R (2005) Legal institutions and financial development. In: Menard C, Shirley M (eds) Handbook of new institutional economics. Springer, Dordrecht

Cochrane JH (2011) How did Paul Krugman get it so wrong? Econ Aff 31:36–40
Dearing JW, Greene SM, Stewart WF, Williams AE (2011) If we only knew what we know: principles for knowledge sharing across people, practices, and platforms. Transl Behav Med 1:1–12
Frey T (2012) Workerless businesses-an explosive new trend: dancing with the inner entrepreneur. J Environ Health 75:46–47
Fugar FD, Agyakwah-Baah AB (2010) Delays in building construction projects in Ghana. Australas J Constr Econ Build 10:103–116
Garrett JW, Teizer J (2009) Human factors analysis classification system relating to human error awareness taxonomy in construction safety. J Constr Eng Manag 135:754–763
Goh RBH (2001) Ideologies of 'upgrading' in Singapore public housing: post-modern style, globalisation and class construction in the built environment. Urban stud 38:1589–1604
Halek M, Eisenhauer JG (2001) Demography of risk aversion. J Risk Ins 68(1):1–24
Hagcvik S (1999) Career consultant: responsible risk taking. J Environ Health 62:29
Hussein A, Megdadi Y, Mohammed A (2010) The value of maps concept for knowledge management based on marketing personnel's view of Jordanian commercial banks. Eur J Econ Finance Adm Sci 26:126–135
Imriyas K, Low SP, Teo AL, Chan SL (2008) Premium-rating model for workers' compensation insurance in construction. J Constr Eng Manag 134:601–617
Karkoulian S, Halawi LA, McCarthy RV (2008) Knowledge management formal and informal mentoring. Learn Organ 15:409–420
Khan ZH, Alin TS, Hussain MA (2011) Price prediction of share market using artificial neural network (ANN). Int J Comput Appl 22:42–47
Kjøllesdal K, Welle-Strand A (2010) Foreign aid strategies: China taking over? Asian Soc Sci 6:3–13
Li RYM (2009a) Legal regulations, people's perceptions on law and scope of services provided by firms: a study on dwelling developers in Beijing and Hong Kong, vol 12. The business review, Cambridge, pp 221–226
Li RYM (2009b) The myth of fly-by-night developers in Shanghai and Harbin. Econ Aff 29:66–71
Li RYM (2010) Factors influencing developers' decision to sell housing units with fittings: empirical evidence from China. The University of Hong Kong, Hong Kong
Li RYM (2012) Econometric modeling of risk adverse behaviours of entrepreneurs in the provision of house fittings in China. Australas J Constr Econ Building 12:72–82
Li RYM, Chau KW (2010) An empirical study of brand name, land costs, income and housing availability's impact on residential fittings. In: Hangzhou, China 16th annual pacific rim real estate society conference. Wellington
Li RYM, Poon SW (2011) Using web 2.0 to share the knowledge of construction safety as a public good in nature among researchers: the fable of economic animals. Econ Aff 31:73–79
Logan Bl, Moseley WG (2002) The political ecology of poverty alleviation in Zimbabwe's communal areas management programme indigenous resources (CAMPFIRE). Geofurum 33:1–14
Matthews K, Matthews O (2010) Controlling bankers' bonuses: efficient regulation or politics of envy? Econ Aff 30:72–76
Mingpao (2011) Billionaires decide to leave. http://hk.news.yahoo.com/%E8%BF%91%E5%8D%8A%E5%8D%83%E8%90%AC%E5%AF%8C%E8%B1%AA%E6%93%AC%E7%A7%BB%E6%B0%91-50-%E7%82%BA%E5%AD%A9%E5%AD%90%E6%95%99%E8%82%B2-%E6%8A%95%E8%B3%87%E9%A6%96%E9%81%B8%E7%BE%8E%E5%9C%8B%E9%A6%99%E6%B8%AF-221248277.html. Accessed 6 Oct 2012
Mohan S, Khorana S, Choudhury H (2013) Why developing countries have failed to increase their exports of argricultural processed producrs? Econo Affairs 33:48–64
Naser K, Moutinho L (1997) Strategic marketing management: the case of Islamic banks. Int J Bank Mark 15:187–203

National Bureau of Statistics of China (2010) Quality of transport routes. http://www.stats.gov.cn/tjsj/ndsj/2010/html/P1605E.HTM. Accessed 6 Oct 2012

Pendharkar PC, Rodger JA, Subramanian GH (2008) An empirical study of the Cobb–Douglas production function properties of software development effort. Inf Softw Technol 50:1181–1188

Rasoulinezhad E (2011) Measuring the role of knowledge management processes in the commercial banks of Iran. Electron J Knowl Manag 9:353–364

Tan NL, Lye YH, Ng TH, Li YS (2010) Motivational factors in influencing knowledge sharing among Banks in Malaysia. Int Res J Finance Econ 44:191–201

Tran D, Skitmore M (2002) The impact of culture on international management: a survey of project communications in Singapore. Australas J Constr Econ Build 2:36–47

Tutzauer F, Chojnacki MK, Hoffmann PW (2006) Network structure, strategy evolution, and the game of chicken. Soc Netw 28:377–396

Whalley AE (2011) Optimal R&D investment for a risk-averse entrepreneur. J Econ Dynamics Control 35:413–429

Zou PXW, Zhang G (2009) Comparative study on the perception of construction safety risks in China and Australia. J Constr Eng Manage 135:620–627

Zou J, Zillante G, Coffey V (2009) Project culture in the Chinese construction industry: perceptions of contractors. Australas J Constr Econ Build 9:17–28

Chapter 5
Property, Credit and Business Cycles in Hong Kong

Abstract Hong Kong is a tiny area, but it houses over 7 million people. The scarce land resources and the relatively high demand for housing together push up the prices of residential units in Hong Kong. For many years, the money spent on housing represented a relatively high proportion of annual household expenditures. The upswing or the decline in residential prices affects many of us. Because the economic environment in Hong Kong affects people's purchasing power and the willingness to spend on housing, this chapter firstly reviews the housing market, credit cycles and the macroeconomic situation in Hong Kong, followed by a Hodrick-Prescott Filter analysis of the business and residential pricing cycles in Hong Kong. Lastly, a Pearson's correlation analysis is used to display the relationship between the prices for several types of housing and economic cycles. The results show that the business cycles have a closer relationship with the larger size units than with the smaller size units. Secondly, there is a closer relationship between the housing cycles for class A to C units (smaller size units) than for class D and E units (larger size units).

Keywords Hp filter · Housing market · Hong Kong

5.1 Introduction

The common cycle analysis is important to the real estate market because various types of interactions exist between the real estate, economic and financial sectors (Wang 2003). For example, real estate investment accounts for over 50 % of total private investment and real estate assets represent just slightly less than 60 % of the wealth in the US (almost 70 % of US real estate is residential). In Korea, housing assets make up over 60 % of the total net worth held by all households (Zhang 2011). Aspachs-Bracons and Rabanal (2010) report that there is a significant relationship between economic downturns and housing price declines in a sample of 18 industrialised countries. During the subprime financial crisis in

R. Y. M. Li, *Law, Economics and Finance of the Real Estate Market*,
SpringerBriefs in Economics, DOI: 10.1007/978-3-642-54245-9_5,

2007–2009 (Li 2011b), the crisis led to a drop in sales of newly built residential units (Li 2011a), the question of the correlation between the housing cycle and the business cycle gained in importance. Alongside poor monetary policy (Landais 2010), Many agree that the downturn in housing prices triggered the defaults in the mortgage market in the US United States, which in turn triggered a complex chain reaction that caused the global financial market and the global economy to stumble (Aspachs-Bracons and Rabanal 2010; Igan et al. 2011; Li 2011b, 2012). Some of the previous research, however, argues that while some components of the construction industry stimulate economic growth, others are simply results of economic growth. Likewise, Burinskienė et al. (2011) note that real estate cycles do not fully coincide with general economic cycles. The declines in the real estate market begin and end earlier than economic declines. Moreover, real estate prices tend to rise steadily in the long run. In the US, it is even suggested that the investment of a large amount of financial resources in housing instead of equipment and plants is a misallocation that results in a concomitant drag on GDP (Chen et al. 2011). In view of these concerns, policy-makers are often puzzled as to whether they should formulate their policies to promote housing investment so as to promote economic growth (Chen et al. 2011).

5.2 Property, Credit and Business Cycles

Events, economics and political systems move via cycles that are similar to the natural life-cycle (Reed and Wu 2010). A cycle is different from a trend because it repeats itself, and hence a cycle allows investors to forecast future prices based on historical records (Li et al. 2011). The terms used to describe business cycles are rich in diversity. Nevertheless, there is a tendency towards standardised terms. For business cycles, the "trough" marks the end of a contraction and the beginning of expansion while the "peak" of a business cycle marks the end of an "expansion" and the beginning of a "contraction" (Burns 1969). Business cycles manifest themselves in the under- or over-utilisation of the productive resources of an economy (Graff and Sturmy 2012). This sequence of changes is recurrent and the duration of business cycles varies from over 1 year to 10 or 12 years (Reed and Wu 2010). Business cycle was at the forefront of the economic research interest in the 1920 and 1940s. The main driver was the unstable economy and the Great Depression in the 1930s. It seemed like the economic cycle in the 1950 and 1960s was "dead", however, the 1970s' oil crisis revived it (Tkacova et al. 2013). Because the phenomenon of economic expansion, contraction and construction in the business cycle can only be found in a market economy, and not in a planned economy, a business cycle analysis is more or less equivalent to the analysis of the economic processes in a capitalist market (Reed and Wu 2010). There are a few factors that lead to the occurrence of business cycles. Recent years witnessed the role played by nominal price rigidity in shaping the US business cycle (Ireland 2001). Other factors, such as exchange rate volatility lead to sudden shifts in the business cycle (Mirdala 2013a). Cyclical patterns in the real estate markets of different countries are fairly similar; the differences arise primarily from country-specific disturbances stemming from social, cultural or political institutions (Li et al. 2011). Previous research shows that business cycles affect interbank rates (Sinicakova and Sulikova 2013), entrepreneurs' strategies (Ishak et al. 2012), employment (Adnan 2008), persisting fiscal and current account deficits (Mirdala 2013b).

Apart from the business cycle in economics, the real estate cycle also often draws people's attention. The property cycle is defined as the repeated oscillations of a market that continually overshoots and then undershoots its steady state. The cycle reflects a degree of instability in the market and a single economic shock leads the market to oscillate around its steady state (Reed and Wu 2010). In Hong Kong, the housing market experienced a boom when the economy rose sharply from 1978 to 1981. Nevertheless, there was a subsequent decline because of oversupply and excessive speculation from 1982 through 1984; the market revived again during the economic expansion in the late 1980s. The negative real interest rates extended the boom to the early 1990s, which caused fluctuations in house prices. Later, the housing market continued to boom despite the restrictions in mortgage lending announced by the government and the banks in 1992. Speculative activities rose to new heights; even though the government announced a task force to dampen speculation on property prices and land supply, the market picked up again in late 1996. In Singapore, a housing market boom occurred between 1980 and 1984 during a period of rapid economic growth that was followed by the liberalisation of the Central Provident Fund (CPF), which allowed CPF savings to be used for private housing mortgages. Housing prices rose by over 100 % between 1979 and 1983 and then dropped with the bust in 1985, which coincided with Singapore's first general recession since independence. The rapid construction of public housing led to the overheating of the economy in the early 1980s, and the subsequent deceleration in construction occurred simultaneously with a worsening economy. The housing market recovered in 1987 and reached a peak in 1996. This period showed a strong economic recovery alongside the liberalisation of regulations governing the purchase and financing of HDB resale flats (Chen et al. 2004).

Similar to business cycles, different countries have property cycles of different lengths. For example, property cycles in Melbourne over the last half century show a regular repetitive 15 year pattern (Robinson 1998). Between 1879 and 1932, there were 10 business cycles in Germany and 11 in Great Britain and France (Burns 1969). Among the housing cycles in European countries, Belgium's upswing was the longest, lasting for nearly 2 decades. Other countries also experienced prolonged growth, e.g., 11 years in Denmark (Ball 2008). Previous research also shows that the lengths of the expansion or a contraction phases are not consistent within one country. Dalsgaard et al. (2001) find that the business cycle in OECD countries has changed over the past 30–40 years. A number of developments changed the structure of OECD economies, spurred by technological advances and structural reform. Many countries during these years shifted towards a service-based economy, which combined with an improvement in inventory management to reduce the destabilising effect from stock building in the business cycle. The increased openness to trade and a surge in intra-firm and intra-industry trade also contributed to the change in the cycle. In the US, information and communication technologies contributed to an increasing growth trend. For example, between 1854 and 1961, the average length of the business cycle in the US was 49 months (approximately 4 years), with the average expansion and contraction lasted for 30 and 19 months, respectively. During the 10 business cycles from 1919 to 1961, the contractions lasted for 15 months and the expansions averaged 35 months. While the declines during this period ranged from 7 to 66 % and averaged 26 %, the increase in industrial production ranged from 18 to 93 % and averaged 38 % (Burns 1969).

Some previous research shows that the property cycle occurs because construction lags in relation to the changing demand for space, which are driven by the fluctuations of business activity. Developed on the modern market system, the conceptual model links the macroeconomy and the sub-markets of space. Changes in economic activities affect households, firms and other types of entities, which in turn affect the demand for space. These changes signal developers to supply more new space. Unfortunately, the lengthy development process often creates a delay or a mismatch with the rapidly changing market demand. The lag between construction demand and supply has become one of the most popular explanations for property cycles (Reed and Wu 2010).

Another theory that explains the relationship of the property cycle to changes in the macroeconomy lies in credit cycles. While low interest rates can potentially cause expansion, high interest rates can lead to contraction in our economies. Property and credit cycles are strongly connected (Davis and Zhu 2011). Bank lending affects property prices via liquidity effects: the changes in lending attitudes and credit availability have a considerable impact on investment decisions regarding new construction and the demand for real estate, which in turn leads to changes in property prices. It has been widely documented that after deregulation, the floods of money seeking investment opportunities and the competition among financial institutions stimulated a building frenzy in some countries during the 1980 and 1990s. Alternatively, the relationship between economic and property cycles can be viewed as being driven by common economic factors; both types of cycles are largely determined by economic conditions and prospects (Davis and Zhu 2011). Others note that the causes or factors that affect the property cycle vary in different cities and countries (Robinson 1998) as does the linkage between property and business cycles; for example, the post war property cycles in Melbourne are identified and associated with the fundamentals of demand and supply (Robinson 1998). Previous research also demonstrates the close relationship between different types of housing cycles. In Malaysia, the cycles in condominium prices appear to be the most exogenous and lead the house price cycles in the terrace, semi-detached and detached housing categories by one to two quarters (Chung 2011). Farrellya and Sanderson (2005) find that real estate actors behave differently at various points of the business cycle.

5.3 Data

According to the Rating and Valuation Department (2012), not all of the residential transactions are included in the data set. The data exclude the housing transactions from public sector developments, including all units built under the Home Ownership Scheme, domestic units built under the Private Sector Participation Scheme for subsidised sales, and units transacted under other programs such as Mortgage Subsidy, Buy or Rent Option, Urban Improvement and Flat-for-Sale Schemes, Sandwich Class Housing, Government owned quarters, and the Tenant Purchase Scheme. Figure 5.1 shows the residential prices for various property types from 1982 quarter 1 to 2011 quarter 3. Abbreviations for the figures can be found in Fig. 5.2.

The residential prices included in this study are for units defined as independent dwellings with separate bathroom (and/or lavatory) and cooking facilities. They are further divided according to the total floor area (Figs. 5.3).

5.4 Research Method

Given a times series Y_t where $t = 1, 2, \ldots, T$, the Hodrick-Prescott filter (HP filter) can be considered to be an additive decomposition $Y_t = Y_t^c + Y_t^g$, where Y_t^c is a cyclical component and Y_t^g is a trend component. The HP filter estimates the trend component via constrained minimisation (UCLA Academic Technology Services 2012). According to Gallego and Johnson (2005),

$$\frac{1}{T}\sum_{t=1}^{T}\left(\mathrm{Iny}_t - \mathrm{lny}_t^*\right)^2 - \frac{\partial}{T}\sum_{t=1}^{T}\left[\left(\mathrm{Iny}_{t+1} - \mathrm{lny}_t^*\right) - \left(\mathrm{Iny}_t - \mathrm{lny}_{t-1}^*\right)\right]^2$$

where y_t^* is the HP filtered time series generated from the actual y_t. Its counterpart matrix can be written as

$$y^* - \left(1_t + \partial\left(P'P\right)\right)^{-1} y$$

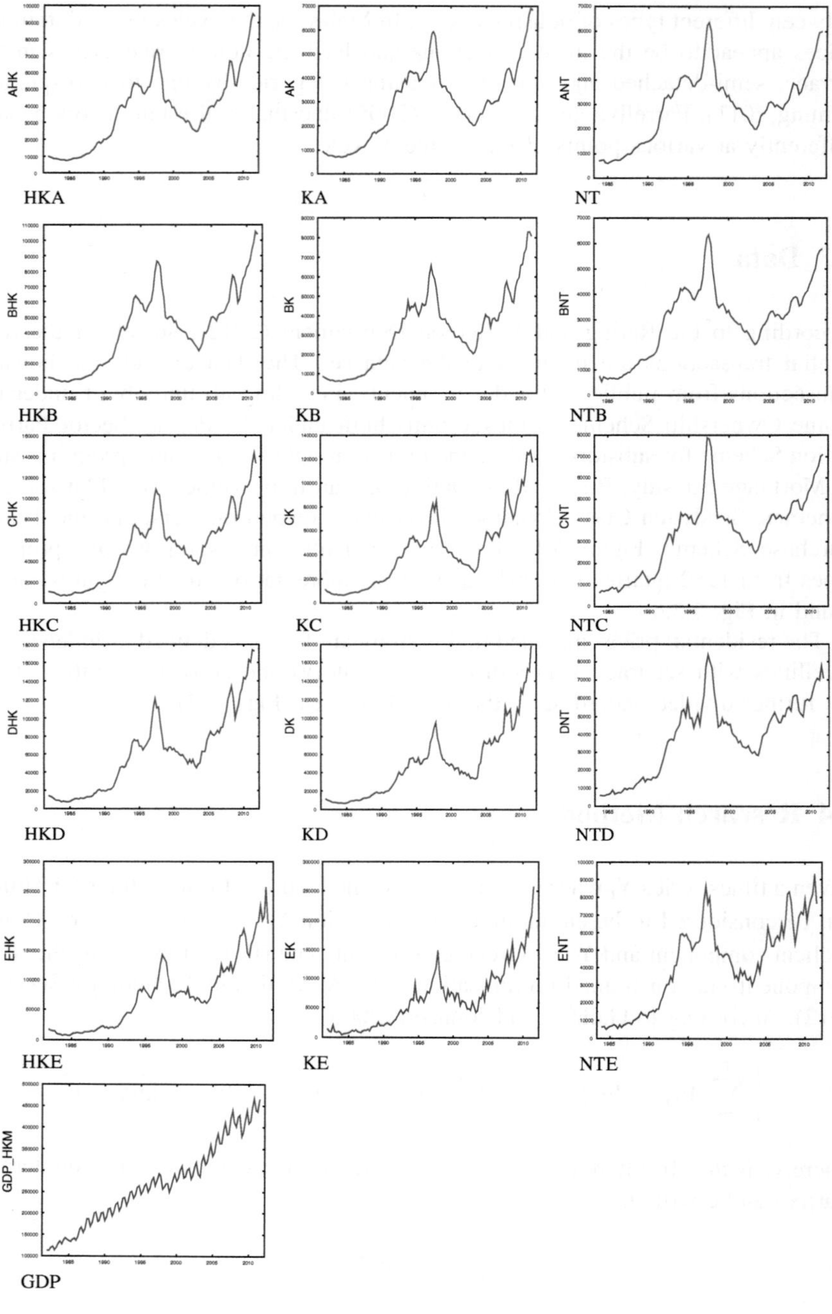

Fig. 5.1 A through E grade housing prices recorded from 1982 to 2011 (author's figure)

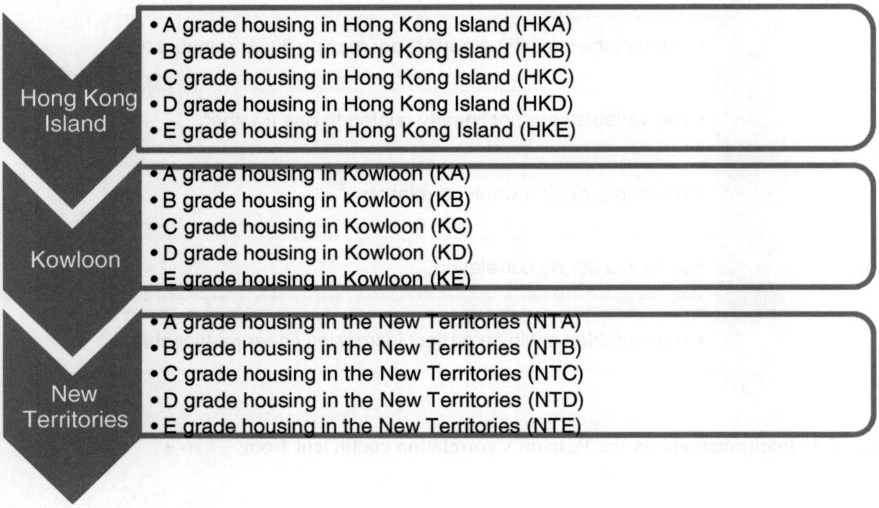

Fig. 5.2 Abbreviations used in this research for different types of housing

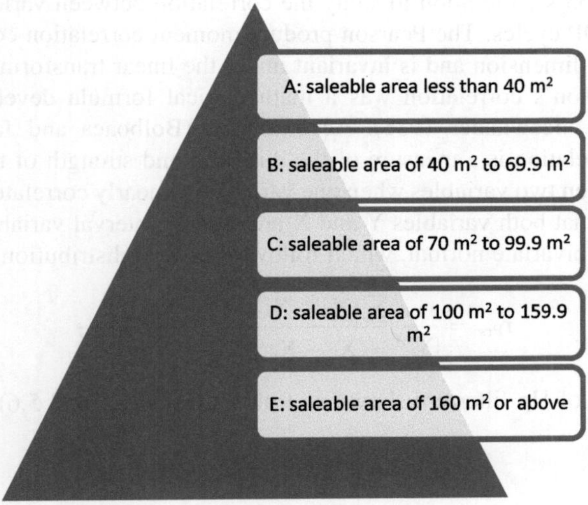

Fig. 5.3 Classifications of residential units in Hong Kong (Rating and Valuation Department 2012)

where P is the T×T matrix represented by a series of concatenated identity and zero matrices, and y and y* are column vectors with dimensions (Y×1):

$$P = \left[1_T \middle| O_{(t-2)\times 2}\right] - 2\left[O_{(t-2)\times 1} \middle| I_{(t-2)} \middle| O_{(t-2)\times 1}\right] + \left[O_{(t-2)\times 2} I_{(t-2)}\right]$$

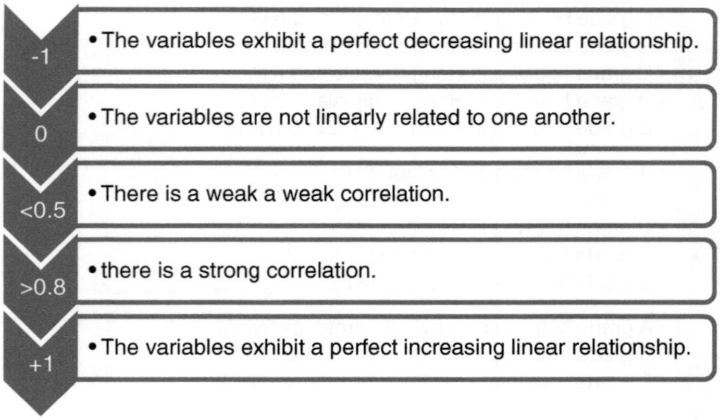

Fig. 5.4 Interpretations on the Pearson's correlation coefficient from −1 to +1

After we obtain the stationary cyclical components of the series using the HP filter, we conduct the correlation analysis, which is similar to the procedure used in the research study conducted by Sayan and Tekin-Koru (2012). This research adopted Pearson's correlation to study the correlation between various residential cycles and GDP cycles. The Pearson product-moment correlation coefficient is an index without dimension and is invariant under the linear transformation of either variable. Pearson's correlation was a mathematical formula developed in 1895 (Rodgers and Nicewander 1988). According to (Bolboaca and Jantschi 2006), Pearson's correlation is a measure of the direction and strength of the linear relationship between two variables when one variable is linearly correlated to the other. It is assumed that both variables Y and X are ratio or interval variables; their joint distribution is bivariate normal, which follows a normal distribution (Fig. 5.4).

$$r_{Prs} = \frac{\sum(X_i - X_m)(Y_i - Y_m)}{[\sum_{i=1}^{n}[(X_i - X_m)^2(Y_i - Y_m)^2]^{1/2}}$$

The results of Hp filter are shown as follows (Figs. 5.5 and 5.6).

5.5 Results

Among the various types of HP housing cycles, there is a stronger relationship between the class A, B, and C housing units (smaller size units) than between the D and E units (larger size housing units). The majority of the correlation values between Class A through E exceed 0.7 at a 99 % significance level. In terms of the relationship between GDP and the housing cycle, all of the types display a positive

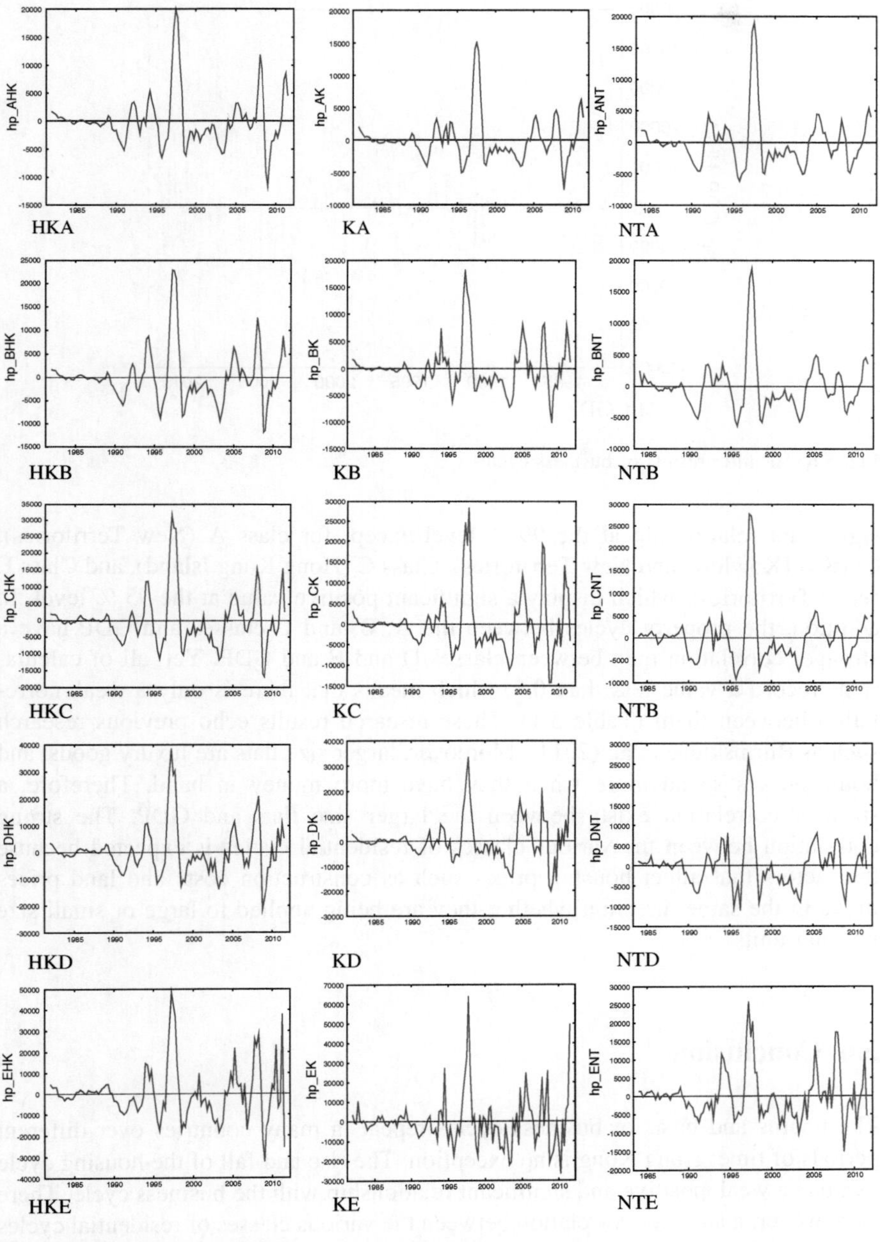

Fig. 5.5 HP filter results of A through E grade housing cycles

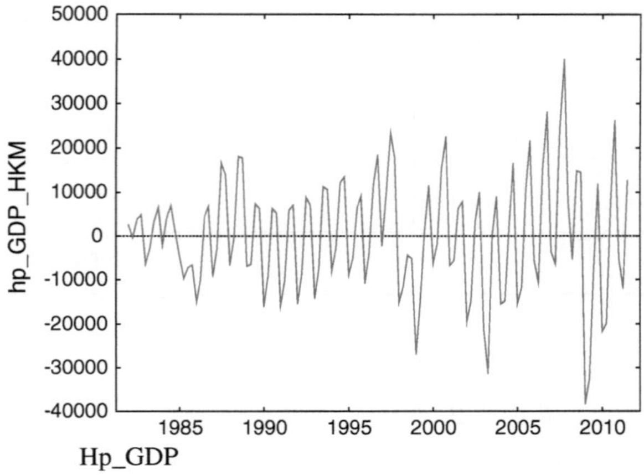

Fig. 5.6 HP filter results of business cycles

significant relationship at the 99 % level except for class A (New Territories), Class B (Kowloon and New Territories), Class C (Hong Kong Island), and Class E (New Territories), which display a significant positive value at the 95 % level. In addition, the property cycles between the A, B, and C classes and GDP have a stronger correlation than between classes D and E and GDP. Yet, all of calculations record a value less than 0.5, which means that there is only a weak correlation between them (Table 5.1). These research results echo previous research such as Burinskienė et al. (2011). Moreover, larger size flats are luxury goods, and home buyers spend more when they have more money in hand. Therefore, a stronger correlation exists between the larger size flats and GDP. The strong correlation between the various classes of residential cycles is expected because the factors that affect housing prices such as construction costs and land prices move in the same direction whether they are being applied to large or small size housing units.

5.6 Conclusion

The booms and busts of business cycles repeat in many countries over different periods of time; Hong Kong is no exception. The rise and fall of the housing cycle exhibits a weak positive and significant relationship with the business cycle. There is, however, a stronger correlation between the various classes of residential cycles because they share similar factors, which leads to the rise and fall in housing prices.

Table 5.1 HP filter results for five classes housing and GDP

	HP_AHK	HP_AK	HP_ANT	HP_BHK	HP_BK	HP_BNT	HP_CHK	HP_CK	HP_CNT	HP_DHK	HP_DK	HP_DNT	HP_EHK	HP_EK	HP_ENT	hp_GDP_HKM
HP_AHK	1	0.970(**)	0.927(**)	0.973(**)	0.907(**)	0.912(**)	0.953(**)	0.886(**)	0.896(**)	0.922(**)	0.841(**)	0.875(**)	0.826(**)	0.715(**)	0.843(**)	0.244(**)
HP_AK	0.970(**)	1	0.965(**)	0.962(**)	0.935(**)	0.957(**)	0.950(**)	0.900(**)	0.945(**)	0.917(**)	0.843(**)	0.909(**)	0.824(**)	0.726(**)	0.821(**)	0.247(**)
HP_ANT	0.927(**)	0.965(**)	1	0.934(**)	0.898(**)	0.990(**)	0.914(**)	0.855(**)	0.971(**)	0.871(**)	0.800(**)	0.909(**)	0.766(**)	0.696(**)	0.771(**)	0.200(*)
HP_BHK	0.973(**)	0.962(**)	0.934(**)	1	0.940(**)	0.935(**)	0.983(**)	0.909(**)	0.918(**)	0.964(**)	0.837(**)	0.923(**)	0.868(**)	0.715(**)	0.878(**)	0.254(**)
HP_BK	0.907(**)	0.935(**)	0.898(**)	0.940(**)	1	0.905(**)	0.939(**)	0.945(**)	0.881(**)	0.912(**)	0.834(**)	0.897(**)	0.838(**)	0.653(**)	0.859(**)	0.200(*)
HP_BNT	0.912(**)	0.957(**)	0.990(**)	0.935(**)	0.905(**)	1	0.918(**)	0.850(**)	0.973(**)	0.879(**)	0.799(**)	0.922(**)	0.773(**)	0.706(**)	0.780(**)	0.220(*)
HP_CHK	0.953(**)	0.950(**)	0.914(**)	0.983(**)	0.939(**)	0.918(**)	1	0.901(**)	0.907(**)	0.961(**)	0.820(**)	0.921(**)	0.880(**)	0.715(**)	0.889(**)	0.224(*)
HP_CK	0.886(**)	0.900(**)	0.855(**)	0.909(**)	0.945(**)	0.850(**)	0.901(**)	1	0.840(**)	0.891(**)	0.829(**)	0.857(**)	0.816(**)	0.646(**)	0.866(**)	0.247(**)
HP_CNT	0.896(**)	0.945(**)	0.971(**)	0.918(**)	0.881(**)	0.973(**)	0.907(**)	0.840(**)	1	0.877(**)	0.791(**)	0.925(**)	0.783(**)	0.710(**)	0.778(**)	0.250(**)
HP_DHK	0.922(**)	0.917(**)	0.871(**)	0.964(**)	0.912(**)	0.879(**)	0.961(**)	0.891(**)	0.877(**)	1	0.805(**)	0.896(**)	0.881(**)	0.713(**)	0.873(**)	0.304(**)
HP_DK	0.841(**)	0.843(**)	0.800(**)	0.837(**)	0.834(**)	0.799(**)	0.820(**)	0.829(**)	0.791(**)	0.805(**)	1	0.742(**)	0.693(**)	0.787(**)	0.722(**)	0.277(**)
HP_DNT	0.875(**)	0.909(**)	0.909(**)	0.923(**)	0.897(**)	0.922(**)	0.921(**)	0.857(**)	0.925(**)	0.896(**)	0.742(**)	1	0.830(**)	0.618(**)	0.858(**)	0.250(**)
HP_EHK	0.826(**)	0.824(**)	0.766(**)	0.868(**)	0.838(**)	0.773(**)	0.880(**)	0.816(**)	0.783(**)	0.881(**)	0.693(**)	0.830(**)	1	0.589(**)	0.845(**)	0.269(**)
HP_EK	0.715(**)	0.726(**)	0.696(**)	0.715(**)	0.653(**)	0.706(**)	0.715(**)	0.646(**)	0.710(**)	0.713(**)	0.787(**)	0.618(**)	0.589(**)	1	0.598(**)	0.396(**)
HP_ENT	0.843(**)	0.821(**)	0.771(**)	0.878(**)	0.859(**)	0.780(**)	0.889(**)	0.866(**)	0.778(**)	0.873(**)	0.722(**)	0.858(**)	0.845(**)	0.598(**)	1	0.220(*)
hp_GDP_HKM	0.244(**)	0.247(**)	0.200(*)	0.254(**)	0.200(*)	0.220(*)	0.224(*)	0.247(**)	0.250(**)	0.304(**)	0.277(**)	0.250(**)	0.269(**)	0.396(**)	0.220(*)	1

* represents statistical at 0.1 level and ** represents statistical significant at 0.05 level

Acknowledgments This chapter is a revised version of a paper Li, Rita Yi Man (2012) Hodrick-Prescott Filter Analysis on Residential Market and Macro Economy in Hong Kong, 7th Annual Conference of The Asian Studies Association of Hong Kong, 2nd–3rd March 2012.

References

Adnan H (2008) An assessment of risk management in Joint Venture Projects (JV) in Malaysia. Asian Soc Sci 4:99–106

Aspachs-Bracons, O. and P. Rabanal, 2010: The drivers of housing cycles in Spain. SERIEs J Span Econ Assoc **1**:101–130

Ball M (2008) House price cycles: evidence from recent European experience 2008. Blackwell Publishing, Oxford

Bolboaca S-D, Jantschi L (2006) Pearson versus Spearman, Kendall's Tau correlation analysis on structure-activity relationships of biologic active compounds. Leonardo J Sci 9:179–200

Burinskienė M, Rudzkienė V, Venckauskaitė J (2011) Effects of quality of life on the price of real estate in Vilnius City. Int J Strateg Prop Manag 15:295–231

Burns AF (1969) The business cycle in a changing world. In: Burns AF (ed) The nature and causes of business cycles. National Bureau of Economic Research, New York

Chen J, Guo F, Zhu A (2011) The Housing-led growth hypothesis revisited: evidence from the Chinese provincial panel data. Urban Stud 48:2049–2067

Chen MC, Kawaguchi Y, Patel K (2004) An analysis of the trends and cyclical behaviours of house prices in the Asian markets. J Prop Invest Finance 22:55–75

Chung HH (2011) Cycles in landed and non-landed housing sub-markets in Malaysia. Int J Hous Markets Anal 4:144–154

Dalsgaard T, Elmeskov J, Park CY (2001) Ongoing changes in business cycle—evidence and causes. In: 23rd SUERF Colloquium (Societe Universitaire Europeenne de Recherches Financieres), Brussels

Davis EP, Zhu H (2011) Bank lending and commercial property cycles: some cross-country evidence. J Int Money Finan 30:1–21

Farrellya K, Sanderson B (2005) Modelling regime shifts in the city of London office rental cycle. J Prop Res 22:325–344

Gallego FA, Johnson CA (2005) Building confidence intervals for band-pass and Hodrick-Prescott filters: an application using bootstrapping. Appl Econ 37:741–749

Graff M, Sturmy J-E (2012) The information content of capacity utilization rates for output gap estimates. CESifo Econ Stud 58:220–251

Igan D, Kabundi A, De Simone FN, Pinheiro M, Tamirisa N (2011) Housing, credit, and real activity cycles: characteristics and comovement. J Hous Econ 20:210–231

Ireland PN (2001) Sticky-price models of the business cycle: specification and stability. Journal of Mone't Econ 47:3–18

Ishak S, Omar ARC, Ahmad A (2012) Tales of the survivors: the Bumiputera Entrepreneurs' experience. Asian Soc Sci 8:25–33

Landais B (2010) The monetary origins of the economic and financial crisis. J Appl Econ Sci 13:280–291

Li RYM (2011a) Imperfect Information and Entrepreneurs' Choice on Provision of House Fittings. Lex Et Sciential Econ Series 18:269–276

Li RYM (2011b) A statistical review on the uneven impact of subprime financial crisis on global property market. In: Macao international symposium on accounting and finance 2011, Macau, China

Li RYM (2012) Chow test analysis on structural change in New Zealand housing price during global subprime financial crisis. In: 18th annual Pacific Rim real estate society conference, Adelaide

Li J, Chiang YH, Choy L (2011) Centralelocal conflict and property cycle: a Chinese style. Habitat Int 35:126–132
Mirdala R (2013a) Current account adjustments and real exchange rates in European transition economies. J Appl Econ Sci 8:210–227
Mirdala R (2013b) Fiscal imbalances and current account adjustments in the European transition economies. J Appl Econ Sci 8:323–352
Rating and Valuation Department (2012) Property market statistics. http://www.rvd.gov.hk/en/publications/pro-review.htm. Accessed 19 Feb 2012
Reed R, Wu H (2010) Understanding property cycles in a residential market. Prop Manag 28:33–46
Robinson J (1998) An investigation of the fundamentals in property cycles. RICS, London
Rodgers JL, Nicewander WA (1988) Thirteen ways to look at the correlation coefficient. Am Stat 42:59–66
Sayan S, Tekin-Koru A (2012) Remittances, business cycles and poverty: the recent Turkish experience. Int Migr 50:e151–e176
Sinicakova M, Sulikova V (2013) Interbank interest rate transmission in the Baltic countries. J Appl Econom 8:372–380
Tkacova A, Banociova A, Sinicakova M (2013) Composite leading indicators of economic cycles in Poland and Slovakia. J Appl Econ Sci 8:240–254
UCLA Academic Technology Services (2012) What does Cronbach's alpha mean? http://www.ats.ucla.edu/stat/spss/faq/alpha.html. Accessed 20 Aug 2012
Wang P (2003) A frequency domain analysis of common cycles in property and related sectors. J Real Estate Res 25:325–346
Zhang W-B (2011) Economic growth with space and fiscal policies with housing and public goods. J Econ Stud 38:452–482

Chapter 6
Should We Abandon the Concept of Artistic Craftsmanship in the Copyright Act in Australia?

Rita Yi Man Li and Yi Lut Li

Abstract In many buildings, such as hotels, shopping malls, it is to common find some statutes and other artistic work. The absence of a definition for a work of artistic craftsmanship creates significant problems in Australia's legal sector. Some people even believe that it would be better to abandon artistic craftsmanship in the Copyright Act. This chapter begins with a review of artistic craftsmanship in the Copyright Act, followed by a study of the possibility of replacing this protection with other legal rules and regulations. This study concludes that the inclusion of artistic craftsmanship contains some value in Australia in spite of the inherent problems.

Keywords Artistic craftsmanship · Work of artistic craftsmanship · Copyright act Australia

6.1 Introduction

Creativity, knowledge and innovation are the basic premises for knowledge economy (Soon 2011; Li 2012; Kim and Chang 2013). Correlative thinking includes analogy, intuition and imagination (Li 2010). This ability is useful to generate useful and novel solutions to solve everyday problems (Lew and Cho 2013). Financial markets, for example, are dynamic processes of entrepreneurial creativity (Soto 2009). Intelligent technologies also require creativity (Jang and Hong 2013). Recognising the importance of creativity in human capital, Thailand has been focusing on the ways to develop people's creativity (Chalapati 2008). In

R. Y. M. Li (✉)
Sustainable Real Estate Research Center, Department of Economics and Finance,
Hong Kong Shue Yan University, Hong Kong, Hong Kong SAR
e-mail: ritarec1@yahoo.com.hk

Y. L. Li
School of Law, City University of Hong Kong, Hong Kong, Hong Kong SAR
e-mail: lliyilut@yahoo.com.hk

R. Y. M. Li, *Law, Economics and Finance of the Real Estate Market*,
SpringerBriefs in Economics, DOI: 10.1007/978-3-642-54245-9_6,

Fig. 6.1 Example of artistic craftsmanship: a model in Adelaide's South Australian Museum (author's photo)

Korea, Robot simulation has been used to enhance learners' creativity (Kim and Seo 2013). In fact, creativity is strongly associated with artistic activity that appears to exceed the automatic routines of behavior and thought that dominate everyday lives (Bain 2005). In modern society, creative and innovative ideas require the presence of private property rights (usually link with good legal systems) (Li 2009; Li and Li 2013). They state clear who has the right to use, derive income and exchange the proper (Li 2009). They also protect the creativity of the artistic work. According to Pila (2009), artistic work means:

1. A drawing, engraving, painting, sculpture, or photograph whether the work is of artistic quality or not;
2. A model of a building or a building, whether the model or building is of artistic quality or not; or
3. A work of artistic craftsmanship where neither of the last two preceding paragraphs applies (Pila 2009) (Fig. 6.1).

Nevertheless, there is no definition for artistic craftsmanship (item 3) in the Copyright Act in Australia. It creates significant difficulties within the legal sector. On the surface, it appears to be simpler to merge "artistic craftsmanship" with the other categories of artistic works in the Copyright Act (s10(1) of the Copyright Act) or to consider it together with designs. Yet, "artistic craftsmanship" should be preserved for several reasons. This chapter begins with a review of the recent case Burge v Swarbrick ((2007) 72 IPR 235), followed by an analysis of the possibilities and the demerits of removing the category of artistic craftsmanship from the Act.

6.2 The Inherent Problem of a "Work of Artistic Craftsmanship" (Hereafter WAC): There is no Definition Provided by the Copyright Act

6.2.1 The Swarbrick Case

Mr. Swarbrick intended to and did include some elements of aesthetic quality in the type JS9000 yachts. Swarbrick alleged that Burge infringed the copyright in the hull, the deck mouldings and the plug. Because he had not registered the design, he could not rely on the Designs Act. The mass production of the yacht prevented him from seeking copyright protection for artistic work except for under the category of a WAC (s77 of the Copyright Act). Hence, Swarbrick argued that the plug and the mouldings of the yacht were a WAC.

Several difficulties arose. First, most products are currently designed for utilitarian purposes. If the design is dictated by function but not by aesthetic value, the work cannot be identified as a WAC because it is primarily functional, not artistic (*Coogi Australia Ltd v Hysport International* (1998) 41 IPR 593). The courts are left with a "question of degree"—how much of an artistic element is there in the product design, and how much is dictated by function?[1]

The Act has not provided any instruction for this question.[2] As evidenced in the judgment on the case, what is considered "aesthetic" and the relevance of functional, utilitarian constraints varies for different subject matters. Moreover, as noted in the Hensher case, [T]here are no absolute standards [for a WAC] as there can be no scientific precision in measurement. Nor can there be unanimity in conclusion though a general consensus of opinion among those whose views command respect will surely be firm ground on which judgment… can be based (*George Hensher Ltd Appellants v Restawile Upholstery (Lancs.) Ltd*, [1976] A.C. 64, Lord Morris).

---

[1] *Swarbrick*, para. 83. Neither the court referred to the decision of *Cuisenaire v Reed* [1963] V.L.R. 719 made by Pape J at p. 729. One of the court decisions shows that the Act was not intended to protect works of craftsmanship but only works created by a particular type of craftsmanship. The inclusion of the adjective 'artistic' requires that the craftsman, in exercising his skill and in the labour of creating the article, must be able to produce something that possesses those attributes suggested by the word.

[2] In the Federal Court, the judges accepted the view that Mr. Swarbrick did put many aesthetic factors in the design and so the moulding, plug and hull of the yacht represented artistic craftsmanship and were protected by the copyright law. Despite the differences in determination, both courts did not.

Without doubt, a WAC creates another problem: the courts must review the subject matter in every case because there is no concise definition in the Act. Additionally, there is no way to know in advance whether someone's creation could fall under this category. No one can know whether their design should be registered—note that registering a design under the Designs Act is a less advantageous option.[3]

A WAC might create a third problem that originates from the abovementioned issues. In Swarbrick, Mr. Hood, the specialist for the defendant, commented that some specialists might not be able to distinguish between an "aesthetic" and a "utilitarian" product element (*Swarbrick*). Even worse, judges are not dictionaries; they must reply on specialists' knowledge and interpretation. Yet, this case illustrates that a specialists' opinion might be unreliable and inaccurate. Adopting their comments and ideas to determine whether a particular object is a WAC might be risky and inappropriate.

6.2.2 Other Case Law

Before Swarbrick came into judgment, several cases involving the WAC issue had already demonstrated the difficulty of interpreting the definition of a WAC. In some common-law jurisdictions, the courts must consider whether the designers intended to include aesthetic qualities in their products. Yet, intent-based tests of copyright protection encourage 'subterfuge' by authors. This subterfuge may mislead the court when deciding whether a work should be a WAC and thereby granted copyright protection.[4] (Note that Swarbrick did not adopt this test.)

6.3 Possibility of Removing the Category of WAC

6.3.1 Can Other Categories of Artistic Work Take Over the Regime of the WAC?

In theory, the answer to the above question is "YES". In the Explanatory Memorandum to the Bill concerning the Designs Act, the following was stated:

[The] amendment clarifies that a work can be both a work of artistic craftsmanship and an artistic work under paragraph (a) or (b) of the definition of 'artistic

[3] Under ss. 46 and 47 of the Designs Act, the maximum period of protection to the author is 10 years. Meanwhile, the period of protection provided by the Copyright Act is for the entire life of the author up to 70 years after the author's death. With the shorter period of protection, applying for a design protection might be less advantageous.

[4] United Kingdom, Report of Copyright Committee, Cmd 8662 (1952) at 236.

work'. For example, a sculpture can be a work of artistic craftsmanship notwithstanding that it is also an artistic work under paragraph (a).[5]

The possible overlapping of the regimes of sculpture and a WAC implies that some 3-D objects might still be protected by the Copyright Act even if the WAC category is removed from the Act. This rationale can be applied to 'engraving', which includes an 'etching, lithograph, product of photogravure, woodcut, print or similar work'.[6] From this viewpoint, the WAC could be eliminated.

6.3.2 Can the Designs Act Take Over the Job?

S7 of the Designs Act provides, inter alia, that a 'visual feature, in relation to a product, includes the shape, configuration, pattern and ornamentation of the product…'[7] Therefore, whether the subject matter is a 2-D object (which is quite uncommon)[8] or a 3-D object, it is still protected by intellectual property law as long as the design is new[9] and distinctive[10] compared to the prior art base.[11] The Designs Act could potentially take over the regime of the WAC.

6.4 Reasons for Keeping the WAC in the Copyright Act: Practical Considerations Involved

6.4.1 The Deficiency of the Designs Act

Theoretically speaking, anything could be registered as a design and its author could receive protection from the Designs Act. In reality, for artistic work as

[5] Designs (Consequential Amendments) Bill 2002 (Cth), House of Representatives, Explanatory Memorandum at 2.

[6] s10(1) Copyright Act. Both sculpture and engraving concern some 3-D objects.

[7] Note that "shape" and "configuration" refer to 3-D subjects and "pattern" and "ornamentation" refer to 2-D subjects.

[8] In *Cuisenaire v Reed* [1963] V.L.R. 719, Pape J. interpreted the word 'craftsmanship' by referring to the Shorter Oxford Dictionary as a 'calling requiring special skill and knowledge especially a manual art—a handicraft.' It is obvious that in most cases, the object of craftsmanship should be some type of 3-D object.

[9] See s16(1) of the Designs Act. A design is new unless it is identical to a design that forms part of the prior art base for the design.

[10] See s16(2) of the Designs Act. A design is distinctive unless it is substantially similar in overall impression to a design that forms part of the prior art base for the design.

[11] s9 of the Designs Act. For the definition of the prior art base, please see s15(2) of the Designs Act.

referred to in the Copyright Act, the author would not be allowed to register the design of his/her work under s18 of the Designs Act if the following apply:

1. an application is made by, or with the consent of, the owner of that copyright for registration of a corresponding design;
2. the design is not to be treated… (as) new and distinctive.

This definition means that if an author wishes to obtain any protection for a WAC, when a novel idea comes into his/her mind, s/he should not materialise the idea until s/he has registered the designs/idea. Is this order of events reasonable?

For some well-recognised examples of a WAC, such as pots, pottery and glassware (*Cuisenaire v Reed* [1963] V.L.R. 719) the specialists might create the product immediately after the novel idea appears. The specialist may come across new idea and change their minds during the process. In this scenario, could the authors possibly submit the application for the designs in advance? Can the Registration Office tolerate the frequent submission of changes of design? Keeping the WAC in the Act is actually a pragmatic consideration.

Note that in s15(2) of the Designs Act, only new and distinctive designs can be registered, meaning that if an author creates a product independently (while he is not subconsciously influenced by other similar designs)[12] and his/her design is not new and distinct from the prior art base, he cannot receive protection except for copyright. Meanwhile, for copyright to subsist in a work, it must be original, but not novel. There is no restraint on individual at all.

Nevertheless, such a creation might not fall into any categories except as a WAC. In other words, no protection or right would be given to the author, as explained in the next paragraph.

6.4.2 The Deficiency of the Copyright Act

Because the other categories of artistic work in the Copyright Act, except for painting, are provided with precise and exact definitions, it is possible that some objects are not covered by any categories for artistic work.

Take the subject matter (a WAC) in the Coogi case (*Coogi Australia Ltd v Hysport International* (1998) 41 IPR 593)—XYZ fabric and garment—as an example. This object does not fall within 'sculpture' because it was not a cast or a model (s10(1) of the Copyright Act); it might be a cutting but not a woodcut, and therefore, it was not an 'engraving' (s10(1) of the Copyright Act); it was not a 'drawing' either[13] (but a drawing of garment-like products are protected by this

---

[12] Otherwise, s/he might be sued by the copyright owner of the product. See *Bright Tunes Music Corp v Harrisongs Music Ltd* 420 F Supp 177 (SD, NY, 1976); *Larrikin Music Publishing Pty Ltd v EMI Songs Australia Pty Ltd* (2010) FCA 29.

[13] s10(1) of the Copyright Act provides, inter alia, that a drawing includes a diagram, map, chart or plan.

category).[14] The presence of WAC is a must to provide complete protection to the authors of artistic work and thereby encourage creation.

6.4.3 Guidance for Interpreting a WAC

Undoubtedly, the lack of a definition for a WAC creates difficulties for the courts when giving judgment. Nevertheless, case law provides useful guidance that mitigates the difficulties that the courts have had in interpreting the concept of a WAC: In Hensher (*George Hensher Ltd Appellants v Restawile Upholstery (Lancs.) Ltd*, [1976] A.C. 64, Lord Morris), "where the main purpose of an article is utilitarian, the less likely is it to be the product of artistic craftsmanship" has been an important note in decision-making. Later, in the Swarbrick case, the court replaced the emphasis on artistic intent with an emphasis on artistic quality instead. Moreover, the court also made clear that the concepts of craftsmanship and aesthetic appeal should not be addressed separately but should be construed as a whole (*Swarbrick* at 66)—it is appropriate to note that Swarbrick makes it easier for the courts to interpret the WAC category in the Copyright Act because a more objective standard was adopted.[15]

6.4.4 Policy Considerations

Not all citizens know the intellectual property law. Some citizens may use a design before making any registration. The presence of a WAC allows the courts to protect the authors with discretion. For example, when a 3-D product is applied industrially (usually 50 pieces, according to Regulation 17 of the Copyright Regulation), it is not an infringement to copyright to reproduce the product. Meanwhile, because the design has been applied before any previous registration, the author is not allowed to receive any protection from the Designs Act (s18 of the Designs Act). The remaining relief is to argue the subject matter, as a WAC is an exception to s77 of the Copyright Act. In addition, if a work is special, it may not be fair to give its author protection of only 10 years (as stated in ss. 46 and 47

---

[14] *Bernstein v Murry* [19821] RPC 303. This idea can be traced from the legislature in the Report of the Gregory Committee from the United Kingdom.

[15] As mentioned in United Kingdom, Report of the Copyright Committee, Cmd 8662 (1952) [236], intent-based tests of copyright protection encourage 'subterfuge' by authors. It would be more difficult and subjective to construe whether the author has such an intention than to include the aesthetic concern when making the design of the subject matter concerned. See also Pila, Justine, 'Works of Artistic Craftsmanship in the High Court of Australia: The Exception as Paradigm Copyright Work' (2008), 36 FLR 3, 372.

of the Designs Act). The author deserves a longer protection period, i.e., the life of the author plus 70 years after his death as provided by the Copyright Act.[16]

6.5 Conclusion

A WAC sounds redundant upon first consideration. Yet, a WAC plays an important role in protecting an author's intellectual property rights. However, it still might be useful to provide some indicators to help make a determination, as suggested by Dr. Kendall Walton.[17] Note that the discussion here evidences the beauty of the common-law system: court cases help to improve the development of our regulations.

References

Bain A (2005) Constructing an artistic identity work. Employ Soc 19:25–46

Chalapati S (2008) Sufficiency economy as a response to the problem of poverty in Thailand. Asian Soc Sci 4:3–6

de Soto JH (2009) The fatal error of solvency II. Econ Aff 29:74–77

Jang H, Hong S (2013) Study on the OSMU (One-Source Multi-Use) management for smart devices. Int J Smart Home 7:1–7

Kim JY, Chang H (2013) A study on performance evaluation of the human resources training program. Int J Smart Home 7:221–229

Kim YJ, Seo YH (2013) Simple programming language for creating a simulation environment with mobile robots. Int J Smart Home 7:3–6

Lew KH, Cho J (2013) Creativity analysis for smart specialist of the ubiquitous era. Int J Smart Home 7:183–193

Li RYM (2009) Private property rights, legal enforcement and economic prosperity: the fall of early civilized China and the Rise of United Kingdom in 18–19th Century. Asian Soc Sci 5:10–15

Li RYM (2010) Traditional Chinese thinking, sustainable development and property management. Real Estate and Dev Econ Res J 2:70–86

[16] s77 of the Copyright Act. This view can be construed from the United Kingdom, The Report of the Gregory Committee at p. 260, quoted in *Swarbrick* 72 IPR 235 at 348: "It may be impossible, and certainly would be unwise, to attempt any exhaustive and fully predictive identification of what can" and cannot amount to "a work of artistic craftsmanship" within the meaning of the Copyright Act as it stood after the 1989 Act.

[17] Kendall Walton, 'Categories of Art' (1970) 79 PHR 344, 349. The article includes some suggested questions such as "Is the work better or more interesting when perceived in the relevant category of work than when perceived in alternative ways?" "Is the matter recognized by the society in which it was created as falling within the relevant category? "Is there a relatively large number of features standard with respect to the relevant category in the work concerned?" "Did the author of the work intend or expect the subject matter to be perceived within the relevant category of work?"

Li RYM (2012) Knowledge management, sharing and creation in developing countries' banking industries. Adv Netw Commun 1:13–26

Li RYM, Li YL (2013) The relationship between law and economic growth: a paradox in China Asian. Social Science 9:19–30

Pila J (2009) Works of artistic craftmanship in the high court of Australia: the exception of paradigm copyright work. Fed Law Rev 36:363–379

Soon TT (2011) Knowledge management enablers, process and organizational performance: evidence from Malaysian enterprises. Asian Soc Sci 7:186–202

Chapter 7
An Offer, An Invitation to Treat and Transaction Costs

Yi Lut Li and Rita Yi Man Li

Abstract While packages of potato chips, bottles of drinks and shampoo on the supermarket shelves are classified as an invitation to offer, medicine in the pharmacy is classified as an invitation to treat. Why are products with a different nature classified differently? This chapter proposes that transaction costs provide the answer to the question.

Keywords Offer · Invitation to treat · Invitation to offer · Transaction costs · Asymmetric information · Institutional economics

7.1 Introduction

An offer is an indication made by one person to another of his or her willingness to enter into a contract. The terms of an offer must be clear enough to allow a contract to be formed by acceptance without further negotiation. An offer can be made to the world at large or to one person only. A purported offer that does not demonstrate these elements will be classified as an invitation to treat. An invitation to treat cannot become a binding contract through acceptance of its terms, but it generally indicates a willingness to negotiate a contract (Christensen 2001). The Pharmaceutical Society of Great Britain v Boots Cash (Chemist) Ltd ([1953] 1 Q.B. 401) laid down a milestone in determining that the display of goods on the shelves in a self-service shop was an invitation to treat but not an offer. Nevertheless, Professor Jill Poole

Y. L. Li
School of Law, City University of Hong Kong, Hong Kong, Hong Kong SAR
e-mail: lliyilut@yahoo.com.hk

R. Y. M. Li (✉)
Sustainable Real Estate Research Center, Department of Economics and Finance, Hong Kong Shue Yan University, Hong Kong, Hong Kong SAR
e-mail: ritarec1@yahoo.com.hk

R. Y. M. Li, *Law, Economics and Finance of the Real Estate Market*, SpringerBriefs in Economics, DOI: 10.1007/978-3-642-54245-9_7,

Fig. 7.1 An invitation to offer in Hong Kong's supermarket (author's photo)

holds an opposing view; she suggests that, with the associated cost savings obtained by the adoption of a self-service system, the display of goods may constitute an offer (Clipsal 2013). Indeed, every judgment should be made in accordance with 'law in actions' and not just the 'law in book'—reality and the best interests of society should be considered. Sellers can maximise their profits by minimising the associated transaction costs, resulting in different points of view on the invitation to treat and offer. Thus, the display in self-service stores can be an offer on some occasions but an invitation to treat on others.

7.2 Invitation to Treat and Offer

We often identify soya source on display in a supermarket (Fig. 7.1), potato chips in CVS Pharmacy (Fig. 7.2), and a book in a bookstore (Fig. 7.3) as an invitation to offer. A contract is made when a person takes the good down from the shelf and goes to the cashier to pay for it. However, the medicine sold in a pharmacy (Fig. 7.4) is considered to be an invitation to treat. The pharmacist has the ultimate decision as to whether he or she will sell the goods or not.

An invitation to treat "is an expression of willingness to negotiate. A person making an invitation to treat does not intend to be bound as soon as it is accepted by the person to whom the statement is addressed" (Abedin 2011, p. 5). An offer is "an expression of willingness to contract on the specified terms without further

Fig. 7.2 An invitation to treat in CVS Pharmacy near Virginia Polytechnic and State University in the US (author's photo)

Fig. 7.3 An invitation to treat in Kaizo-sha in Tokyo (author's photo)

Fig. 7.4 Medicine put on the shelves in a Hong Kong pharmacy is invitation to treat (author's photo)

negotiation" and only it is "capable of immediate translation into a contract by the fact of acceptance" (Clipsal 2013).

7.3 Asymmetric Information, Transaction Costs and Risk Aversion

The main issue pointed out by Akerloff in 1970 about markets is the information asymmetry between the buyers and sellers (Li 2010). The buyers know about their own trading behavior and the quality of the products they are selling but the sellers can at best guess at what the buyers know from information gathered about them, such as their reputation and trustworthiness. Trading partners use each other's' reputations to decrease information asymmetry so as to facilitate trusting trading relationships (Mui et al. 2002). As transactions involve uncertainty about their outcome (Li 2008), such kind of imperfect information affects market power, prices and leads to a dis-equilibrium, asymmetric information is a market failure which undermines the product transactions efficiency (Li 2012). The problem of asymmetric information causes significant frictions in the transmission mechanism of monetary policy (Tas 2011), workers' mobility and contracts for credit (Tsoulouhas 1996).

One important feature between the product seller and the buyer in a grocery shop, pharmacy and supermarket is asymmetric information too. The buyer wishing to buy medicine knows more about his illness or medical condition than the seller. While selling an apple to the wrong person may not have any consequence, selling medicine to those who are not in need may constitute a fatal consequence or a legal suit. As Bajari and Tadelis (2013) comment "an important aspect of contractual arrangements is their ability to accommodate adaptation, thus creating a tradeoff between transaction costs that are due to changes and incentives to reduce costs." This comment implies that the difference between an invitation to treat and an offer lies in (1) the associated transaction costs of the contractual arrangement and (2) risk aversion behaviour of human beings.

Transactions are the basic unit of organisational analysis, involving a contract to transfer goods or services from one party to another (Memili et al. 2011). Transaction cost theory was pioneered by Coase and developed by Williamson. It is based on the postulation that firms are profit maximizers and human beings are haviour occasionally in pursuit of these objectives (Qu and Brocklehurst 2003). In utility maximizers, agents are boundedly rational and display opportunistic be a broader sense, transaction costs can be considered to be the "costs of running the economic system" (Memili et al. 2011). Transaction cost theories concentrates on dark side of human nature, sheds light on the dishonesty rather than incompetence. It raises the concern of false information embodied in promises and contracts (Li 2010). Partly because of the existence of asymmetric information, we have to take risks in many of the decision makings. The notion of risk taking, i.e. the will to carry out actions with an uncertain outcome (Sauner-Leroy 2004), however, is not the same among us. For example, boys/men scores higher than girls/women (Vermeersch et al. 2013). No matter what, urban service delivery decisions must confront scale and externality problems and other transaction risks (Feiock et al. 2010). The decision of identifying goods display on shelves as an offer or an invitation to treat is of no exception.

7.4 The Boots Case

Under the Pharmacy and Poisons Act 1933s 18(1), sellers of drugs listed in the schedule of poisons were required to supervise their customers at the point where the 'sale is effected'. The defendant adopted a self-service system, allowing the shoppers to pick the drugs off the shelves and to pay at the counter where the pharmacists would supervise the sale; no pharmacist stood in front of the shelves to supervise the selection of drugs. Thus, fewer pharmacists were employed and the operation costs could be reduced. The plaintiff claimed that the display of drugs constituted an offer and that once the consumers picked the drugs off of the shelves, there was an acceptance. Hence, no supervision was provided at the venue where 'the sale is effected'.

7.4.1 *Judgments*

Judges supported the judgment (1952) ([1952] 2 Q.B. 795) and held that the display on shelves was only an invitation to treat but not an offer (*Boots* (n1) Somervell LJ). Self-service stores allowed the customers to choose and to substitute. Offers were made by the consumers when they bought the goods at the cashier. If the display was an offer, the buyer would be bound to buy the drug once he had taken it off of the shelf. The buyer would not be allowed to make substitutions. This procedure was impractical; hence, the defendant's appeal was dismissed.

7.4.2 *Arguments Supporting the Judgment of the Boots Case*

The judgment was made in accordance with the judgment of *Grainger and Son* v *Gough* ([1896]) A.C. 325, 334, H.L.(R), which agreed that the price list does not amount to an offer because it was impossible for the defendant to supply an unlimited amount of wine; therefore, the price-list was only an invitation to treat. Applied to the *Boots* case ([1953] 1 Q.B. 401), price cards and the display of drugs in the self-service shop should not be treated as an offer; otherwise, the seller would be held to numerous contractual obligations to supply the goods, which it would be quite unable to carry out. Indeed, as Carlsson mentioned, the sellers are interested in maximising the amount of sales, and psychological studies show that the conditions under which the buyers were bound to buy would result in far fewer sales (O.C Carlsson–'Juristische Rundschau', 1954). Hence, from a socioeconomic viewpoint, which is the concern of the law, it is unreasonable to hold the display of goods in a self-service store as an offer that binds the shopper to purchase any good that they pick up off of the shelves.

7.5 Poole's Finding

Courts say that the display of goods is an invitation to treat when they intend to reserve the right to refuse to sell. In this way, the action of the buyer paying at the cashier's counter is an offer and the acceptance can only be committed by the seller.

Poole argued that with the associated cost saving, the display of goods under a self-service system is a standing offer. Costs are saved because the sellers no longer need to employ shopkeepers to stand in front of each shelf to supervise every sale. Instead, the transaction takes place at the cashiers, who addresses the selling of goods from all around the shop, and thus fewer workers are needed. Hence, the cost of operation and the distribution of goods are reduced. However, this arrangement may lead to a loss of freedom of contract. Poole drew this conclusion by referring to the *Chapelton* Case ([1940] 1 K.B. 532): "…for the convenience of the local authority (lessor) the public (lessee) were asked to obtain from the chair attendants tickets… (lessee) obtained his receipt at the same time as he took his chair… This was a general offer to the general public…there would be an obligation upon (lessee) to search out the attendant, like a debtor searching for his creditor…".

From the above judgment, it is possible for Poole to make the analogy that once a buyer obtains the goods, he must accept and pay for the offer. That is why the freedom of contract was no longer available to the seller. The offer ends when the stock is exhausted, i.e., it is a standing offer. Moreover, whether the contract is made depends on whether the customers buy the goods. Hence, the control of the contract and its acceptance would rest with the customer.

7.6 Display as an Invitation to Treat

It may be wrong to conclude that an offer is made when the goods are picked up off the shelves. It is "more realistic to say that the customer has not passed beyond the stage of preliminary negotiation until the goods are taken to the cash desk" (Montrose 1955). For example, it is possible that the price cards may have become mixed. Hence, the true reason for treating the display as an invitation is that the sellers are intent on reserving their right to refuse to sell, and thus they provide an opportunity to correct mistakes and protect their best interests.

7.7 Extension

In reality, the display of goods being treated as an offer is found more commonly when involving automated (vending) machines. In *Thronton v Shoe Lane Parking*, Lord Denning MR said,

> The customer pays his money and gets a ticket. He cannot refuse it. He cannot get his money back. He may protest to the machine, even swear at it. But it will remain unmoved. He is committed beyond recall…the offer is made when…the machine…as being ready to receive the money. The acceptance takes place when the customer puts his money into the slot. ([1971] 2 Q.B. 163).

This condition is further developed in the *City Parking Services v Murray* et al. case (1991 St. J. No. 1755). Although the plaintiff employed neither an attendant nor an automated system for collecting fees—he just put signs that were objectively visible to ask for payment from those who used his parking lots—Cameron J. still held that "parking was being offered under specified terms; one could accept the offer by parking without further communication with the owner."

Moreover, it is possible to argue that the consumer's act of picking up a good may not constitute an offer because the intention to accept must be clearly and finally demonstrated, e.g., the act of boarding a bus; while the picking up of goods can have many implications, and the display of goods allows the customer to pick a good up for examination while reserving the right to make substitutions (Unger 1953).

7.8 Display in the Self-Service Shop as an Offer

Boots Ltd. is a large-scale retailer operating in the self-service mode. Boots is similar to the chain supermarkets currently selling ordinary goods in Hong Kong, making it necessary to investigate whether displays in supermarkets are an offer or an invitation to treat.

As mentioned in the previous paragraphs, the picking up of goods by customers may form either an invitation to treat or an offer. Hence, to determine the nature of the display in supermarkets, it is better to see whether the supermarkets are willing to surrender their rights to refuse to sell at the cashier counter.

It is not surprising that sometimes the prices shown on the price cards do not coincide with the computer's reading. In such cases, the supermarkets generally sell the goods according to the price on the cards rather than that stored in the computer systems. The supermarkets will generally allow customers to buy at the lower prices that they saw. In this way, supermarkets can be treated as automated vending machines with human beings acting as the mechanics. No negotiation occurs. Though customers can ask the shopkeepers to void the items that have been read by the register, it makes no difference. Supermarkets should be considered to be upgraded vending machines in which the items do not go out immediately when the customers press the button; there is a confirmation process that allows the customers to refuse to buy until a final acceptance is made, i.e., the seller's collection of payment.

The reason that supermarkets are willing to sacrifice their rights to refuse to sell and negotiate the price with customers is that, although selling at the lower prices stated on the price labels on shelves will result in a lower revenue, the supermarkets accept the cost to preserve their reputation and keep their customers. To survive, supermarkets actively advertise and cut prices to attract customers. These steps are far more costly than the loss committed by abandoning their right to refuse to sell (negotiate), and so supermarkets are willing to surrender their right to refuse to sell. In short, in supermarkets selling ordinary goods, the display is an invitation to treat.

In the *Boots* case ([1953] 1 Q.B. 401), the display should be treated as an invitation to treat because the goods sold were drugs and extraordinary in the sense that any abuse may result in death. If injury or death occurs resulting from the absence of supervision when choosing the drugs, the shop could be held liable for negligence because they lacked sufficient monitoring. In this way, the compensation required would be much greater: the shops need to not only pay the medical costs, but they would need to pay the consequential loss, e.g., wages lost due to an inability to work and compensation for the death. Therefore, even if Boots Ltd. had not been required to employ pharmacists and exercise their right to refuse to sell, the company would still do so. If they abandoned their right to refuse to sell and avoided employing pharmacists, they might need to pay legal costs and subsequent compensation, which are much greater than the pharmacists' wages. In this sense, the display must be an invitation to treat, and not an intent to bind the customers to buy what they pick up. The true reason is that Boots, being a reasonable store, would never surrender its right to refuse to sell.

7.9 Conclusion

Judgments highlight the importance of reasonableness and should be changed according to different situations. The display of goods in self-service stores may constitute an offeror's invitation to treat. Poole's theory holds when the self-service stores sell ordinary goods but not in the cases when dangerous items are involved. The authors speculate that the underlying reason is due to transaction costs. Whilst the costs of selling potato chips to a wrong person are quite low, the costs of selling a wrong medicine to a wrong person can be very high.

Acknowledgments This chapter is a revised version of a book chapter previously published in Li, Rita Yi Man (2011) Everyday life application of Neo-institutional Economics Lambert Academic Publishing, Saarbrucken, Germany. The author would like to thank the publisher for granting the right to republish with substantial changes.

References

Abedin B (2011) Web 2.0 and online learning and teaching: a preliminary benchmarking study. Asian Soc Sci 7:5–12

Bajari P, Tadelis S (2013) Incentives versus Transaction Costs: a theory of procurement contracts. Rand J Econ 32(3): 387–407

Christensen S (2001) Formation of contracts by email—is it just the same as the post? QUT Law Justice J 1:22–38

Clipsal (2013) Smart home technology. http://www.clipsal.com.au/. Accessed 24 March 2013

Feiock RC, Lee IW, Park HJ, Lee KH (2010) Collaboration networks among local elected officials: information, commitment, and risk aversion. Urban Aff Rev 46:241–262

Li RYM (2008) Nature of the firm: a study on developers in China and Hong Kong. J Appl Econ Sci 3:479–486

Li RYM (2010) Factors influencing developers' decision to sell housing units with fittings: empirical evidence from China. The University of Hong Kong, Hong Kong

Li RYM (2012) Econometric modeling of risk adverse behaviours of entrepreneurs in the provision of house fittings in China. Australas J Constr Econ Build 12:72–82

Memili E, Chrisman J, Chua JH (2011) Transaction costs and outsourcing decisions in small- and medium-sized family firms. Fam Bus Rev 24:47–61

Montrose JL (1955) The contract of sale in self-service stores. Am J Comp Law 4:235–239

Mui L, Mohtashemi M, Halberstadt A (2002) A computational model of trust and reputation for e-business. In 35th Hawaii international conference on system science (HICSS 35 CDROM). IEEE Computer Society, p.1–10

Qu Z, Brocklehurst M (2003) What will It take for China to become a competitive force in offshore outsourcing? An analysis of the role of transaction costs in supplier selection. J Inf Technol 18:53–67

Sauner-Leroy J-B (2004) Managers and productive investment decisions: the impact of uncertainty and risk aversion. J Small Bus Manage 42:1–18

Tas BKO (2011) An explanation for the price puzzle: asymmetric information and expectation dynamics. J Macroecon 33:259–275

Tsoulouhas T (1996) Labor and credit contracts with asymmetric information and bankruptcy. Eur Econ Rev 40:1665–1682

Unger J (1953) Self-service shops and the law of contract. Mod Law Rev 16:369–372

Vermeersch H, T'Sjoen G, Kaufman J-M, Houtte MV (2013) Social science theories on Adolescent risk-taking: the relevance of behavioral inhibition and activation. Youth Soc 45:27–52

Chapter 8
The Effect of the Global Subprime Financial Crisis on the Macroeconomy and the Housing Market in the UK

Rita Yi Man Li and Lokki Mak

Abstract The housing bubble's boom and bust made a significant contribution to the financial crisis, prompting a chain reaction that spread throughout the world. These events raised the eyebrows of investors worldwide. In this chapter, the author investigates the impact of the financial crisis on the UK's macroeconomy and housing market.

Keywords Subprime financial crisis · Housing market · US · UK

8.1 Introduction

Housing price is affected by a number of factors. Home buyers wish to pay less for houses in heavy rainfall regions and higher price for one-degree-Celsius rise in temperature. Previous research estimated an increase in price of 298.28 pounds per dwelling for a one-degree-Celsius increase in mean annual temperature (Li 2009, 2011a, 2012c). Zhang and Chen (2011)'s research showed that there the Central Bank Reserve Ratio had long term negative impact on the real estate market. Li (2010) suggested that land price was a major determinate of housing prices. Oxley et al. (2008) proposed that housing quality can also be an important factor which determines the housing price. Others found that environmental pollution (Li 2012b) and financial crisis led to a drop in housing prices (Li 2011b, 2012a, d). This chapter aims to reveal the subprime financial crisis on the UK housing market. In 1970, the UK experienced an economic crisis; however, the impact of the 2007 financial crisis on the UK's macroeconomy and its housing market was

R. Y. M. Li (✉) · L. Mak
Sustainable Real Estate Research Center, Department of Economics and Finance, Hong Kong Shue Yan University, Hong Kong, Hong Kong SAR
e-mail: ritarec1@yahoo.com.hk

R. Y. M. Li, *Law, Economics and Finance of the Real Estate Market*, SpringerBriefs in Economics, DOI: 10.1007/978-3-642-54245-9_8,

significantly larger. The real estate market worsened and the UK entered into an economic recession. In this chapter, we propose two research questions:

1. How did the UK real estate market perform during the subprime financial crisis?
2. Why did the US subprime crisis affect the UK's real estate market?

This research will review the impact of the 2007 financial crisis on the economics of the UK real estate market. UK economic and real estate market performance data are then analysed to investigate how the UK was affected by the crisis. The lessons that can be learned in the UK from this crisis will be discovered and included in the conclusions of this chapter.

8.2 Background of the United Kingdom

8.2.1 Analysis of the Macroeconomic Environment

In this chapter, macroeconomic data, such as the gross domestic product (GDP), the unemployment rate, net exports and foreign investment, are good indicators to show economic performance.

There was a clear upward trend in economic growth from 2000 to 2007. Nevertheless, the UK's GDP dropped significantly after the financial crisis from nearly 360,000 million in the third quarter of 2008 to 344,000 million pounds in the first quarter of 2009. This decrease represents approximately a 4 % drop in the GDP. In addition, the unemployment rate ranged from 4.8 to 5.3 % before the financial crisis, as shown in the Fig. 8.1.

During the financial crisis, the unemployment rate started to increase, reaching approximately 8 % by late 2009. Even toward the end of 2008, however, the unemployment rate had escalated beyond its normal level in the UK. The financial crisis had a time lag effect on the unemployment rate, in part caused by the sequel of the financial crisis. More companies became insolvent in 2009, as shown in the Figs. 8.2 and 8.3

However, the export to import ratio in Fig. 8.4 forms a small U-shaped curve. It appears that financial crisis did not have any immediate impact on this ratio: the major trading partner of the UK was the European Union with 27 countries, and the United States was only the UK's second largest partner.

8.2.2 International Investment Position

Because of the financial crisis, foreign investment in the UK dropped (Figs. 8.5 and 8.6). Owing to the time lag problem, this decreasing trend started in the fourth quarter of 2008. The demand in the residential housing market decreased and the residential price decreased.

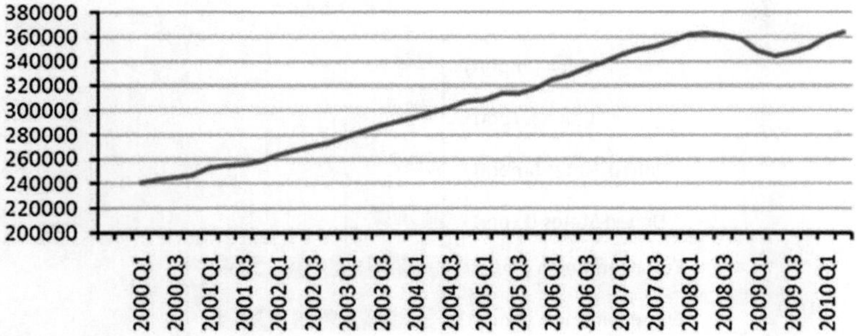

Fig. 8.1 UK gross domestic product (in millions of pounds) 2000–2010 (UK National Statistics 2010)

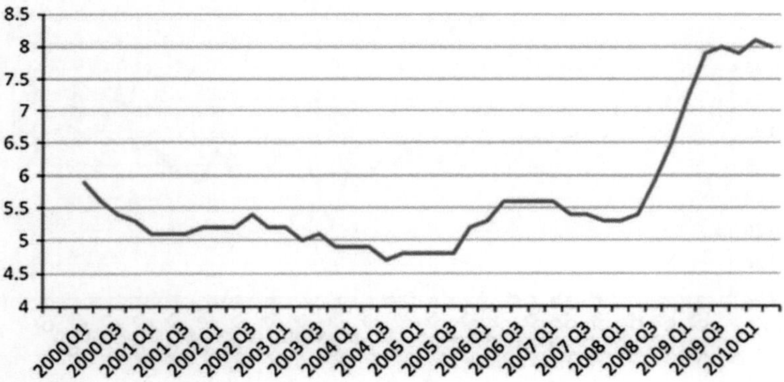

Fig. 8.2 The UK unemployment rate 2000–2010 (UK National Statistics 2010)

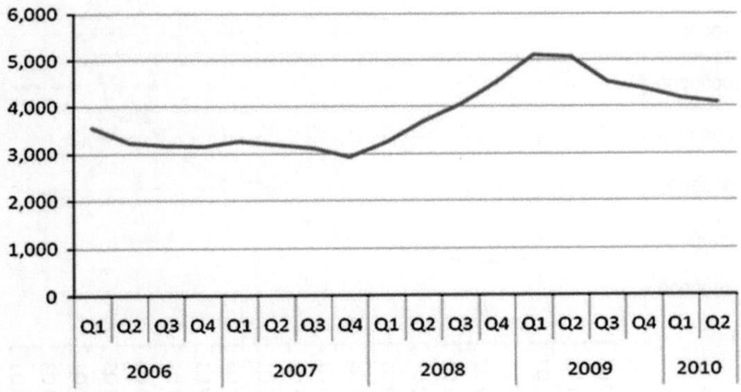

Fig. 8.3 Number of insolvent companies in the UK (HM Government of the UK 2006–2010)

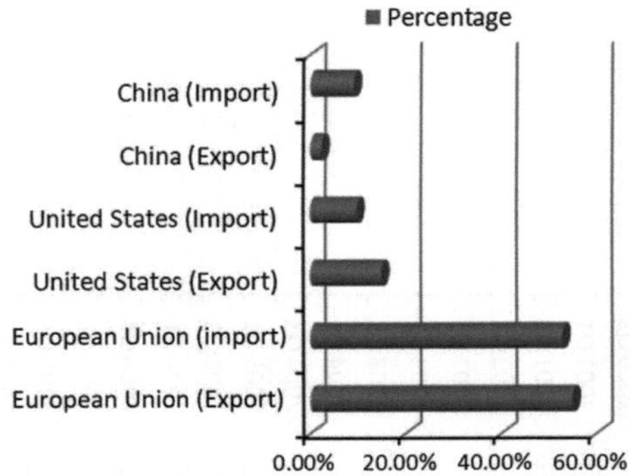

Fig. 8.4 Major trading partners of the UK (World Trade Organization 2010)

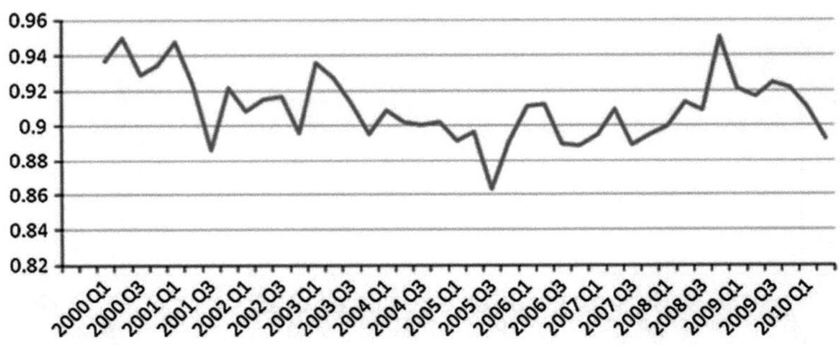

Fig. 8.5 The UK's export to import ratio (UK National Statistics 2010)

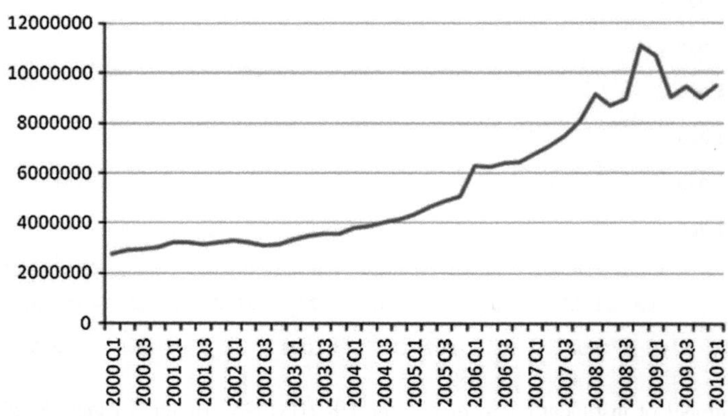

Fig. 8.6 International investment position (UK National Statistics 2010)

8.3 Subprime Financial Crisis

In 2007, the credit markets boomed, boosting the global housing market. Buyers became overconfident in their housing investments (Foo 2008). Banks and building societies could easily expand their lending because there was a credit surplus. There were hundreds of billions of dollars in the housing market (Stiglitz 2008). The existence of financial innovations such as derivatives encouraged lending (Chamberlin 2009), and a bubble formed in the housing market. Bankers packaged the risky assets as a safe assets and resold them (Mishkin 2009). This repackaging decreased people's risk awareness regarding these financial products. The risks were underestimated and credit was excessively expanded; thus, the banking system became highly leveraged and, finally, the subprime mortgage crisis occurred (Chamberlin 2009). The housing market dropped and the housing bubble burst. Many mortgages defaulted, and the related financial products became worthless. The banks and the related financial institutions could not call back these loans; some of these institutions collapsed, and thus, the financial crisis began in the US and spread worldwide.

Many countries suffered in the sharp increase and sudden great drop during this decade. Compared with other developed countries, however, the UK's housing price boom occurred much earlier and its increase was more sustainable. Moreover, the pattern of these housing price increases was fairly uniform in every region of the UK. This uniformity means that the price pattern of a strong growth followed by a sudden fall was similar in all regions (Chamberlin 2009). When analysing the patterns in the US, it can be seen that the price fluctuation trend was different across regions, including various trends even during the same time period. The literature also shows that housing price performance in the UK was slightly different from that in the US and other developed countries. The trends in the real estate crisis in the US, the UK, Spain and Australia vary significantly (Chancellor 2010) because of the national differences in the housing supply. The US had land that was readily available for development, and new construction on this land escalated during the financial boom. The housing supply eventually exceeded the demand. In the UK, the housing price and the housing supply also increased, but it did not keep up with supply as it did in the US.

8.4 Research Methodology

In this research, we use data from before and after the financial crisis to analyse the impact of this crisis on the UK real estate market. The literature will support the data analysis and the findings.

8.4.1 Data Sources

All of the data are collected from the official government websites in the United Kingdom. Different data are found within different official departments. Following are the sources of UK data (Table 8.1).

8.4.2 Data Range

In this chapter, the range of the collected data is approximately 10 years, from the first quarter of 2000 to the second quarter of 2010. Because we must analyse the effect of sub-prime financial risk on the UK's real estate market from 2007 to 2009, a 10-year data analysis is sufficient to cover the economic change related to this crisis. The previous literature has shown that an average business cycle is approximately 6 years, with a range from 2 to 10 years in the UK (Angus 1991). Thus, 10 years of data containing 40 quarters is sufficient for our purposes. The data collected will be used to analyse the market situation in the United Kingdom. All of the data are shown in pounds sterling.

8.5 Data Analysis on UK Housing Market

We can see from the data that the financial crisis had a significant impact on the property market. Examining the residential prices below, the price started to decrease in the third quarter of 2007. This price decrease can be explained by the simple economic theory for the supply and demand of a product.

8.5.1 Demand in the Housing Market

On the demand side, there is no doubt that the demand for property decreased drastically because of the subprime mortgage crisis. Because the demand cannot be derived from an individual resident, it is measured using the transaction volume. The change in the housing price has shown a strong correlation with the number of transactions (Chamberlin 2009). Our figure begins in 2006, it shows a significant drop in the second quarter of 2007. Housing prices then started to increase slightly in early 2009 (Figs. 8.7, 8.8).

Before the financial crisis, there was an upsurge in property buying worldwide, including the United Kingdom. Many first time buyers entered the market. The housing price paid by a first time buyer became significantly higher: in 2000, the average price for a first time buyers was only 60,000 pounds. Because of

Table 8.1 Data sources

Sources	Data
UK National Statistics (2010)	Gross domestic product Unemployment rate Export to Import ratio International Investment position
Nationwide (2011)	Residential price First time buyers housing price First Time buyer affordability index-Mortgage payments as percentage of mean take-home pay
UK HM Revenue and Customs (2011)	Transaction volume The number of insolvent companies
UK Community Department (2011)	Completed dwellings
Bank of England (2011)	Building societies' secured gross lending to individual and housing associations Mortgage rate Lending secured on dwellings
World Trade Organization (2010)	Major trading partners
Federal Housing Finance Agency (2011)	US Housing Price Index

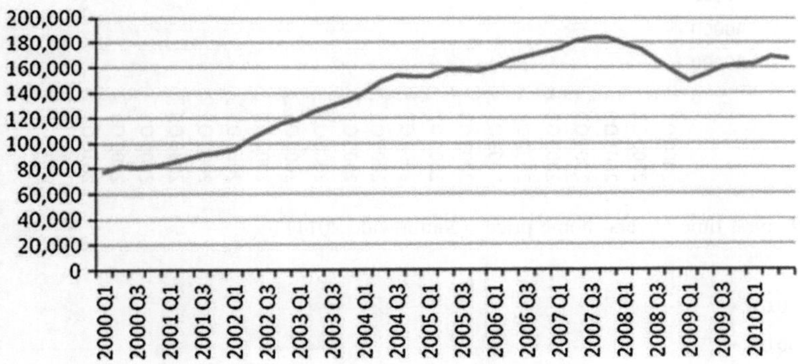

Fig. 8.7 Average residential price in pounds 2000–2010 (Nationwide 2011)

increasing residential prices and the optimistic outlook that most people held towards property prices, many people bought higher priced homes. In the third quarter of 2007, the first time homebuyers' price reached 160,000 pounds, representing a 166 % increase in 7 years (Fig. 8.9).

The first time buyer affordability index shows mortgage payments as percentage of the mean take-home pay. The affordability index can provide some insight on the effect of the housing market developments on a household's financial position and the direction of property prices (Chamberlin 2009). The index below shows mortgage payments as a percentage of mean take-home income (Fig. 8.10).

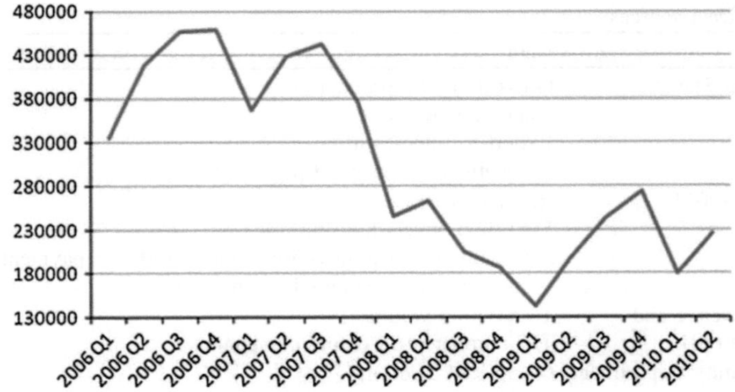

Fig. 8.8 Residential property transaction volume UK (UK Community Department 2011)

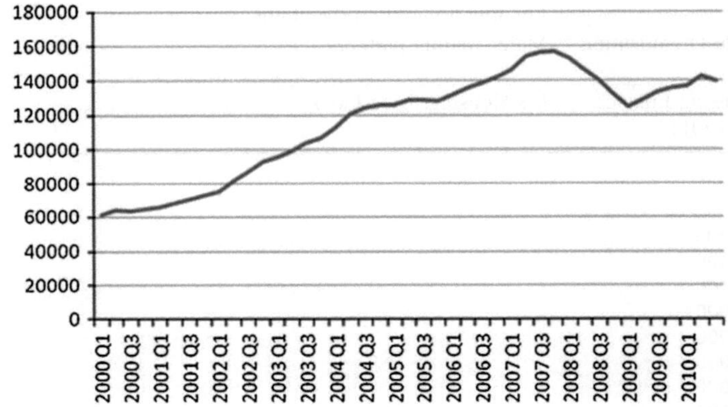

Fig. 8.9 First time buyers' home prices (Nationwide 2011)

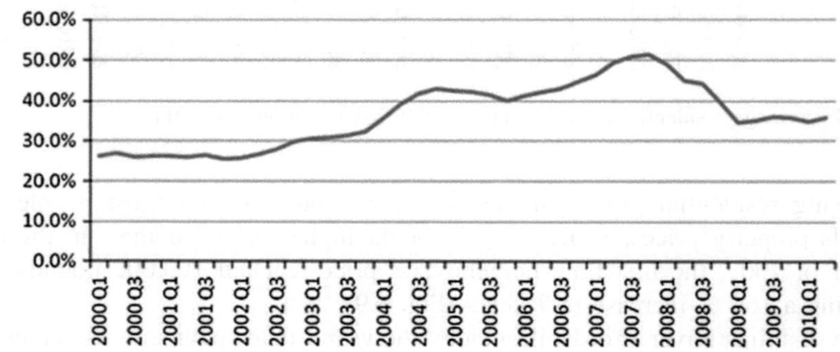

Fig. 8.10 First time buyer affordability index—mortgage payments as percentage of mean take-home pay (Nationwide 2011)

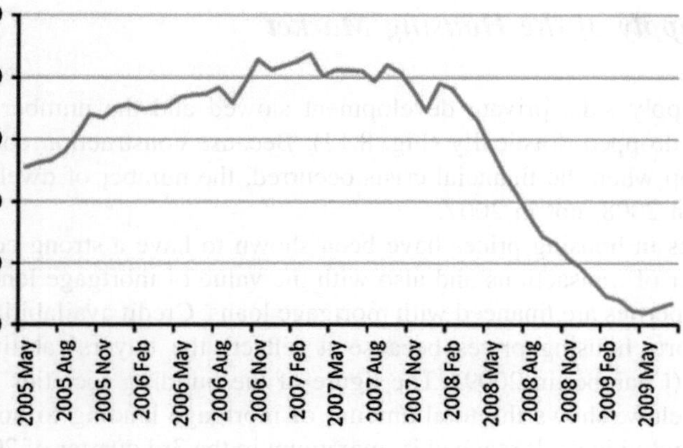

Fig. 8.11 Lending secured on dwellings (million) (Bank of England 2011)

Fig. 8.12 Completed dwellings UK's community department 2000–2010 (UK Community Department 2011)

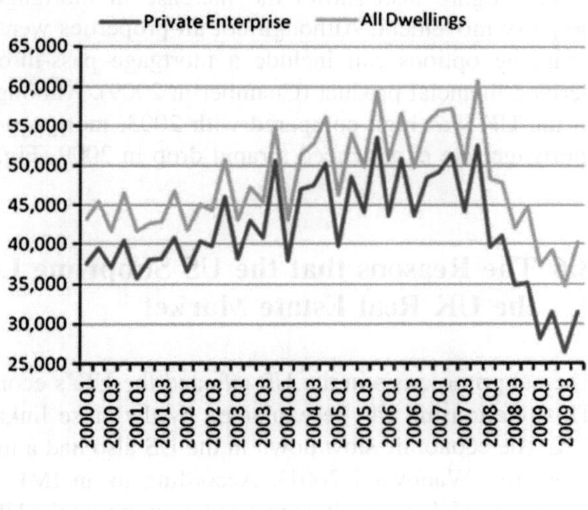

In 2000, the percentage was at 26 %. When the property market became active, the percentage increased, reaching 51 % by the 4th quarter of 2007. At this point, mortgage payments represented approximately half of the buyer's take-home income.

The lending secured on dwellings increased from 2005 to 2007, as shown in the following Fig. 8.11, and then had a significant drop in February 2008. People borrowed money to buy a house and used the house as collateral for their mortgage. These buyers assumed low risk because they could give up ownership if they had no ability to repay the mortgage loan. The demand for lending secured by these dwellings was high while the bubble was forming; when the bubble burst, the amount of lending secured by dwellings decreased sharply (Fig. 8.12).

8.5.2 Supply of the Housing Market

On the supply side, private development slowed and the number of completed dwellings dropped drastically (Fig. 8.12). Because construction could not immediately stop when the financial crisis occurred, the number of dwellings began to decrease in 2008, not in 2007.

Changes in housing prices have been shown to have a strong correlation with the number of transactions and also with the value of mortgage lending, although not all properties are financed with mortgage loans. Credit availability is one factor that supports housing prices because it reflects the buyers' ability to obtain a mortgage (Chamberlin 2009). The figure of the building societies' secured gross lending, below, shows the total amount of mortgage lending to housing associations and individuals. It reached its maximum in the 3rd quarter of 2007 and it then decreased drastically to return to its normal level in 2009. Thus, this chart demonstrates that lending availability boosted housing prices.

This figure also shows the increase in mortgage approvals and the record property movement. Although not all properties were financed using a mortgage, financing options can include a mortgage pass-through, which is a mortgage-derived financial product (Chamberlin 2009). Although the mortgage rate in 2007 in the UK was high compared with 2003, mortgage lending also increased. The mortgage rate experienced a rapid drop in 2009 (Fig. 8.13).

8.6 The Reasons that the US Subprime Lending Affected the UK Real Estate Market

The subprime crisis in the US affected the UK's economy and real estate market. This relationship can be explained by the close linkage between the US and the UK. The economic slow down in the US also had a tremendous impact on the UK economy (Wadhwani 2001). According to an IMF study (2001), the economic cycle of the UK is highly correlated with that of the US. Although the trading share relative to GDP is not large between the US and the UK, the correlation between the UK and the US economies has been higher than that between the UK and the EU since 1960 (IMF 2001). The US had two-fifths of the foreign direct investment in the UK and the UK has one-fifth of the foreign direct investment in the US (Wadhwani 2001). Some sectors that have a downward trend in the US also see a similar trend in the UK. According to the US Census Bureau, the US real estate and financial industries are important elements in its economy (US Census Bureau 2008). In addition, the US is the leading country in the world; a downturn in the US might have an impact on other countries, including the UK. The property and real estate market in the UK were affected by the financial crisis in the US (Fig. 8.14).

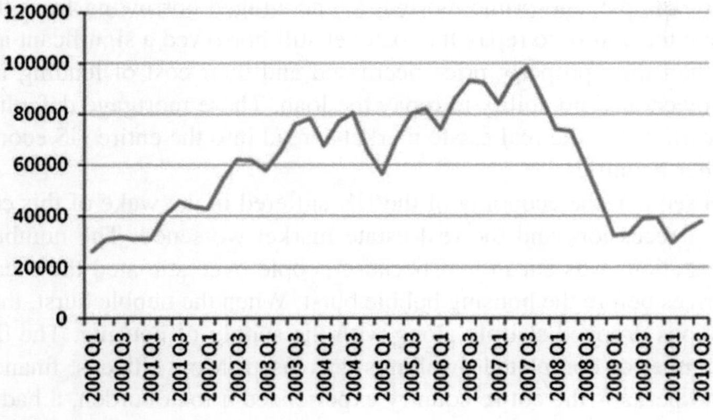

Fig. 8.13 Building societies' secured gross lending to individual and housing associations in millions (Bank of England 2011)

Fig. 8.14 US Housing Price Index (HPI) and UK HPI (Nationwide 2011)

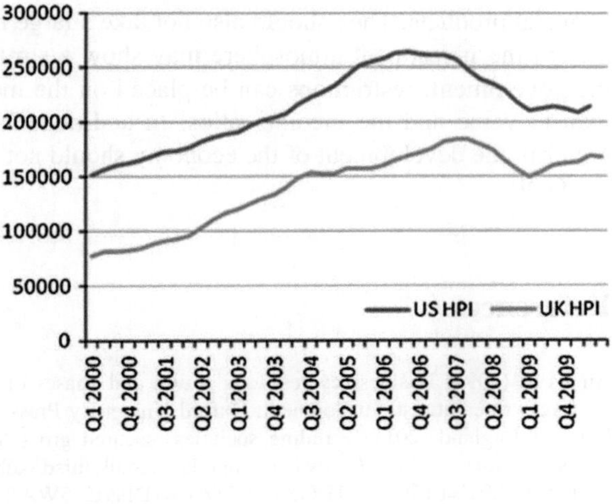

8.7 Conclusion

Financial crises occur frequently. Although the historic financial crises are not all exactly the same, their causes are similar (Chan 2010). The UK has experienced various financial crises and significant drops in the real estate market during different periods. The 2007 subprime mortgage crisis has been an important lesson for the UK. Reviewing the cause of the financial crisis, it is clear that capital and risk in the financial sector need to be managed. The capital in banks was misallocated; there were hundreds of billions of dollars invested in housing (Stiglitz 2008). Mortgage loan sometimes required no documentation in the applications and mortgages were reaching up to 100 % of the home's value.

Moreover, by 2008, there were many innovations in financial products related to mortgage loan. These financial innovations led to financial instability (Chan

2010). For example, sub-prime mortgages encouraged borrowing from those who did not have the ability to repay the loan yet still borrowed a significant amount of money. When their property price decreased and their cost of lending increased, these borrowers had no ability to repay the loan. These mortgage defaults and the ensuing downturn in the real estate market spread into the entire US economy and then to other countries.

We can see that the economy of the UK suffered in the wake of this crisis. The UK faced a recession, and the real estate market worsened. The number of real estate transactions was cut in half because people overestimated the escalation of housing prices before the housing bubble burst. When the bubble burst, the number of transactions dropped sharply along with the supply of housing. The data show that the number of completed dwellings decreased. Most citizens, financial institutions, and perhaps the entire country experienced a loan burden, a bad situation for any economy.

Therefore, a good regulatory system is needed for residential markets and banks to prevent the reoccurrence of a similar crisis. High returns are linked with the high risk. People should not be overconfident regarding the real estate market or other financial products. They should also not take a large mortgage to buy a house even though the investment atmosphere may show a strong market. From the view of the government, restrictions can be placed on the mortgage market that limit the loan to value and the income ratios. In addition, the proportion of the property sector in the development of the economy should not be such a large percentage of the GDP.

References

Angus M (1991) Business cycles, long waves and phases of capitalish development. Dynamic forces in capitalist development. Oxford University Press, New York

Bank of England (2011) Building societies' secured gross lending to individual and housing associations. http://www.bankofengland.co.uk/mfsd/iadb/index.asp?Travel=NIxSTxTAx&levels=1&C=LMR&C=1DG&C=63T&C=1DF&C=5WA&G0Xtop.x=39&G0Xtop.y=6&Nodes=X46527X35672X35914X35916&SectionRequired=A&HideNums=1&ExtraInfo=false#BM. Accessed 20 Aug 2011

Chan TL (2010) Insight: seven lessons of the global financial crisis. http://www.info.gov.hk/hkma/eng/insight/20100324e.htm. Accessed 25 Nov 2010

Chamberlin G (2009) The housing market and household balance sheets, in http://www.ons.gov.uk/ons/elmr/09_09/downloads/ELMR_Sep.pdf#page=24, Accessed on 30 December, 2012

Chancellor E (2010) Why some housing bubbles remain? Financial Times. http://www.ft.com/intl/cms/s/0/b5e074f4-cd88-11df-9c82-00144feab49a.html#axzz2rwTfsVEu

Federal Housing Finance Agency (2011) FHFA resources. http://www.fhfa.gov. Accessed 10 Dec 2010

Foo CT (2008) Conceptual lessons on financial strategy following the US sub-prime crisis. J Risk Finance 9:292–295

Li RYM (2009) The impact of climate change on residential transactions in Hong Kong. J Built Hum Environ Rev 2:11–22

Li RYM (2010) Factors influencing developers' decision to sell housing units with fittings: empirical evidence from China. The University of Hong Kong, Hong Kong

Li RYM (2011a) Building our sustainable cities. Common Ground Publishing, Illinois

Li RYM (2011b) A statistical review on the uneven impact of subprime financial crisis on global property market. In: Macao international symposium on accounting and finance 2011, Macau, China

Li RYM (2012a) Chow test analysis on structural change in New Zealand housing price during global subprime financial crisis. In: 18th Annual pacific rim real estate society conference, Adelaide

Li RYM (2012b) The internalization of environmental externalities affecting dwellings: a review of court cases in Hong Kong. Econ Aff 32:81–87

Li RYM (2012c) A review on 10 countries' sustainable housing policies to combat climate change. In: 18th Annual pacific rim real estate society conference, Adelaide

Li RYM, Li J (2012) The impact of subprime financial crisis on Canada and United States housing market and United States housing cycle and economy. In: ICBMG conference, Hong Kong

Mishkin FS, Eakins SG (2009) Finanial market and institutions. Pearson United States

Nationwide (2011) Residential price. http://www.nationwide.co.uk/hpi/historical.htm. Accessed 24 Sept 2011

Oxley M, Elsinga M, Haffner M, Heijden HVD (2008) Competition and social housing in Europe. Econ Aff 28:31–36

Stiglitz JE (2008) Lessons from the global financial crisis of 2008. Freefall: free markets, and the sinking of the global economy. Norton, New York

UK Community Department (2011) Completed dwellings. http://www.communities.gov.uk/housing/housingresearch/housingstatistics/housingstatisticsby/housebuilding/livetables. Accessed 26 Sept 2011

UK HM Revenue and Customs (2011) Residential property transaction volume. http://www.hmrc.gov.uk/stats/survey_of_prop/menu.htm. Accessed 24 Sept 2011

UK National Statistics (2010) Publication hub. http://www.statistics.gov.uk/StatBase/tsdataset.asp?vlnk=208&More=N&All=Y. Accessed 5 Jan 2013

US Census Bureau (2008) Gross domestic product by industry and state. http://www.census.gov/compendia/statab/2010/tables/10s0656.xls. Accessed 6 Jan 2013

Wadhwani SB (2001) The impact of the US slowdown on the UK economy. Bank Engl Q Bull 41:248–252

World Trade Organization (2010) Statistics database. Major trading partner of UK. http://stat.wto.org/CountryProfile/WSDBCountryPFView.aspx?Language=E&Country=GB,US. Accessed 21 Nov 2010

Zhang J, Chen W (2011) Dynamic impact of interest rate policy on real estate market. Asian Soc Sci 7:188–194

Chapter 9
Changes from the Visible Hand to the Invisible Hand: The Land Market in Hong Kong Before and After the Asian Financial Crisis

Abstract Land is a mandatory factor for production. The method of land disposal is particularly crucial in high-density populated areas. In Hong Kong, the land supply was once constrained by a quota of 50 ha per year under the Joint Declaration. This quota was removed after the return of Hong Kong to mainland China. The Asian Financial Crisis and the implementation of the 85,000 housing policy led to a significant drop in the demand for land. The Lands Department then announced the new land disposal policy, which included a land application system. This policy allows the developer to play a much more active role in the land acquisition process. This chapter mainly focuses on the land market in Hong Kong before and after the introduction of the land application system.

Keywords Visible hand · Land market · Asian financial crisis · Transaction costs · Hong Kong

9.1 Introduction

The relationship between land and housing prices has always been linked with the discussion of flour and bread's pricing relationship. Indeed, all the residential buildings' construction requires the presence of land (Li 2010). Land is scarce in Hong Kong: a tiny area houses over 7 million people. Before the handover of Hong Kong to China, the Lands Department played an active role in land sale via auction and tender. The joint declaration restricted the land supply through a 50 ha limit on disposal every year. The shortage in the land supply maintained the prices at a high level. The so-called high land price policy era began. After the return of Hong Kong to China in 1997, the 50 ha visible hand intervention was removed, and the supply of land increased. It was expected that land prices would fall to a lower level. The Asian Financial Crisis and the 85,000 housing policy, however, led to a great drop in the demand for land. There were several land auctions during which no developers showed an interest in land purchase. The HKSAR government then implemented a

R. Y. M. Li, *Law, Economics and Finance of the Real Estate Market*,
SpringerBriefs in Economics, DOI: 10.1007/978-3-642-54245-9_9,

land sale application system, where the developers take an active role in the land supply. The developers need to express their interest in purchasing a particular piece of land first, providing the price and other information to the Lands Department. The visible hand control of the government (the 50 ha limit) has been changed to an invisible hand (a primarily market-driven land supply).

9.2 An Overview of the Land Market in Hong Kong

The colonial government used the leasehold system to dispose of land. There were 99 and 999 year leases. Occasionally, we can still find freehold land. The land market at that time was imperfect: no developer in Hong Kong knew everything about the market, nor did government officials have all of the information. No stakeholders would search for complete information, they would only search for the information that was optimal for them (Tse 1993). For example, the stakeholders did not identify the maximum price for land, the price at which the developer would no longer buy.

The demand for land in Hong Kong is governed by many factors. The expectation for the future market price and the derived demand, etc., in the case of an increasing land supply has indirectly affected the land demand. After the announcement of an increase in the land supply, the number of housing transactions usually falls significantly. The land price depends on the land's marginal value rather than just the quantity. The marginal value is derived from the demand for housing, which in turn determines the price of residential land. It is therefore not surprising to find that there is an increase in the price of land whenever there is intense competition for its use, for example, in the case of urban land.

There is a direct relationship between the government restriction of the land supply and a high land price. One previous research develops an econometric model to test the relationship between land restrictions and property price. The finding shows that the gradual leasing of land creates the anticipation of a future housing supply. This expectation drives up the current demand for housing and, in turn, pushes up the price (Christine Loh and Citizens Party 1997). Furthermore, the demand for land is a derived demand, derived from the demand for the product that it produces. When a housing shortage is anticipated, an increase in the demand for property leads to an increase in the demand for the land, which in turn pushes up the land price.

9.3 High Land Price Policy Before 1997

Before the handover of Hong Kong to China, there was an annual 50 ha limit on land disposal, which had been included in the joint declaration since 1985. All of the income from land transactions is "taken by the colonial government"

Table 9.1 Revenue from land sales 1985–1997 (Li 1999)

Year	Land area disposed	Government revenue from land sales (HK$ million)	Total revenue (HK$ million)	Percentage of colonial revenue from land sales
1985–1986	58	423	41240	1
1986–1987	55	1863	43869	4
1987–1988	74	2920	55641	5
1988–1989	155	5681	65780	9
1989–1990	78	6354	74365	9
1990–1991	134	2761	82674	3
1991–1992	88	7394	101456	7
1992–1993	164	7459	120780	6
1993–1994	128	16804	143899	12
1994–1995	1410	16150	151052	11
1995–1996	205	16838	153194	11
1996–1997	310	26468	173857	14

(Legislative Council 1997). Before 1997, the Hong Kong Government practiced the so-called high land price policy. The government used its control over the land supply, determining the amount of land to be released on the market each year, to earn major portions of its revenue. In 1995, 32 % of the government's total revenue came from land sales (Christine Loh and Citizens Party 1997). The following table shows the revenue from land sales from 1985 to 1997 (Table 9.1).

Apart from purchasing a piece of land at a land auction, when the developer wants to purchase land for development, there are a number of ways to do so. Developers can obtain land using the following processes:

1. Tender: Government officials determine the successful applicants using a number of factors: the price and the intended land use—whether the land use can fulfil the aim of the government for the use of land. However, the successful applicant is usually the applicant who can pay the highest price. Moreover, the tender is usually made on land that will not arouse public interest, e.g., an gas station.
2. Change in use: The developer who has the land, e.g., farmland in the New Territories, can apply for a change in the land use to develop the property on that piece of land. For example, the YOHO town was originally a piece of farmland; an application was made to convert it to residential land. The Pacifica is another example: it was originally a dockyard. The housing developer applied for a change in land use.
3. Private market: Land can be obtained through purchase from a private landowner, similar to other goods in Hong Kong.

9.4 Abandon Annual 50 ha Limit on Land Disposal

After the return of Hong Kong to mainland China, the 50 ha policy was abandoned, and the authorities elaborated their first land disposal program on 8 October 1997. As part of their program, the government specifically announced that they would increase the amount of available land. In the 1997 policy address (Chief Executive 1997), the Chief Executive placed a major emphasis on this issue. "We have already announced the five year land sales program that will provide 120 ha of land for private housing up to March 1999, and an additional 260 ha of land in the following three financial years. In addition, there will be about 185 ha of land for public housing sectors… to provide more land, we will within the next 10 years develop strategic growth in areas such as Tseng Kwan O and proceed with the Tseun Wan Bay and Green Island reclamation".

This policy change was one of the most significant for Hong Kong land policy since 1997. The change affects the supply, demand and even the role of government in the land market.

9.5 Immediate Market Response to the Removal of the 50 ha Land Restriction

People expected that there would be a substantial increase in the land supply after this policy change and some changes would be seen in the Hong Kong land market after 1997. This section will discuss the changes in the Hong Kong land market.

9.5.1 Price of Land

It is obvious that both a decrease in demand and an increase in supply will push down the price of land. By increasing the supply of land, the use value of the land definitely increased; however, the price, i.e., the exchange value in the land market dropped (Figs. 9.1 and 9.2). This drop occurred primarily because the exchange value of land is determined by its relative scarcity and its marginal value. The famous Paradox of Value, also known as the Water-Diamond Paradox, illustrates this issue: water has a high use value but a low exchange value, and a diamond is the converse. This paradox occurs because the supply of diamonds is so small that the marginal values are very high, while water's supply is so high that marginal value is very small.

Fig. 9.1 Initial supply

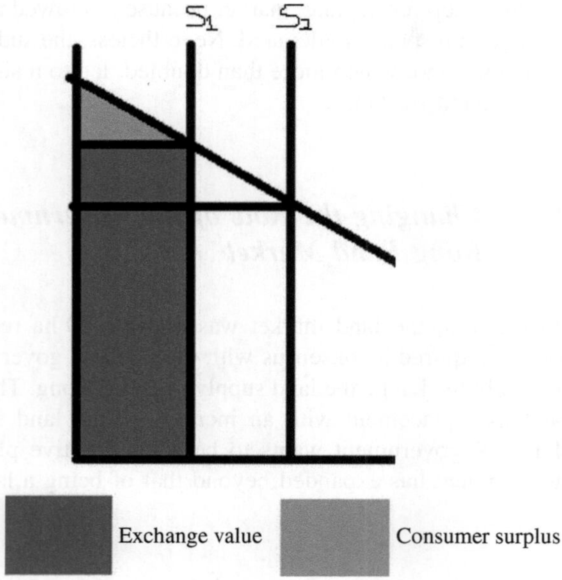

Fig. 9.2 Supply increase

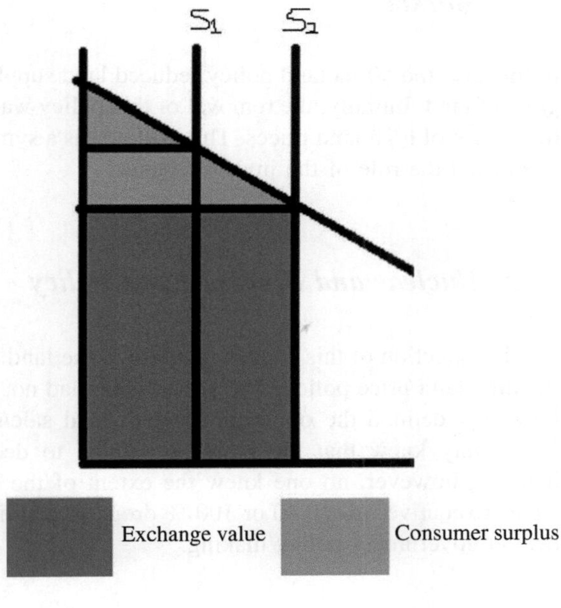

9.5.2 A Change the Market Structure of Leasing Out Land

The amount of land released was originally restricted by the Joint Declaration. There was a restriction on the maximum supply of land. The removal idea was a positive step for the land market because it allowed the government land supply to change in response to demand. Nevertheless, the sudden increase in the amount of available land, which more than doubled, led to a significant drop in the price and the demand for land.

9.5.3 Changing the Role of the Government in the Hong Kong Land Market

In the past, the land market was under a 50 ha restriction, and changes to this policy required a consensus with the Chinese government. Now, the HKSAR has the right to change the land supply in Hong Kong. The removal of the 50 ha policy and its replacement with an increase in the land supply make it clear that the HKSAR government wants to be a more active player and that the role of the government has expanded beyond that of being a land supplier.

9.5.4 The Intervention of the Visible Hand in the Land Market

In the past, the 50 ha land policy reduced land supply and therefore pushed up the price of land. Initially, the removal of this policy was good because it removed the root cause of high land prices. This policy was a symbol of the visible hand, which attenuated the role of the invisible hand.

9.5.5 Unclear and Blurred Land Policy

The introduction of this sudden increase in the land supply also marked the end of the high land price policy. The government had not indicated a clear direction for how they defined the optimum level of land sale/supply. The citizens of Hong Kong only knew that the HKSAR wanted to decrease the price of land and housing; however, no one knew the extent of the price decrease desired by the Chief Executive—a 10, 40 or 100 % drop? In addition, no one knew the rationale behind government policy making.

9.5.6 Increasing the Risk of Investment in the Land Market

Before 1997, the high land price policy gave the impression to investors and developers that land prices would only increase; this increase was the actual market trend at the time. Investors and developers were therefore willing to pay a high land price because they believed that it was nearly impossible to lose money. Investors and developers believed that the rate of return after selling a residential flat would be so high that the revenue could cover the cost. Moreover, the 50 ha land policy ensured that the supply of land was steadily maintained at a low rate. Therefore, the risk of investing in land was negligible. The only concern of investors and developers was getting their hand on the property faster than their competitors! However, the imposition of the new land policy has increased the supply of land and nobody is sure when the HKSAR government will stop this increase, which affects the future property market and so on. This increase in uncertainty regarding the future land market has substantially increased the risk of investing in land.

9.6 Land Application

Because of Tung's announcement of a substantial increase in land sales and because of the Asian Financial Crisis, many land auctions at that time could not attract developers to bid for the land. The government then announced a new Land Application System. First, the developers needed to identify one particular piece of land that they would like to buy and needed to submit a guaranteed bank deposit on the land. Upon receipt of the application, the Lands Department will decide if the offered price is acceptable. If the price is acceptable, the Lands Department will arrange an auction or tender after some major considerations.

1. Auction. If the applicant is successful in acquiring the site, the deposit is used to offset the purchase price. However, if the applicant is not successful in acquiring the site, then the cashier order or deposit cheque will be returned to him on the day just after the auction. However, if the auction does not reach the minimum price, then the deposit will be forfeit.
2. Tender. If the applicant successfully obtains the site in tender, the deposit will be used to offset the purchase price of the land. If not, the deposit cheque will be returned to him within one week after the tender award. However, if the auction does not reach the minimum price, then the deposit will be forfeit (Fig. 9.3).

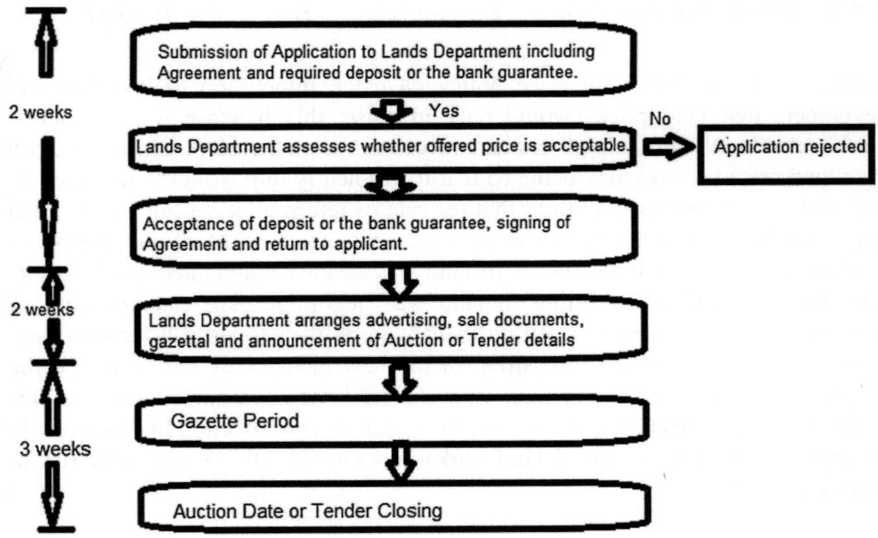

Fig. 9.3 Land application procedure (Lands Department 2007)

9.7 Change in the Role of Government: The Invisible Hand Replaces the Visible Hand

The land market has always been regarded as being dominated by the major supplier, i.e., the government. The government is the largest landlord in Hong Kong. The demand and supply of land is determined by government policy. However, with the introduction of land applications, the developers indicate demand for a particular site by writing to the Lands Department about the location of the land and indicating how much they are willing to pay. The active role of the government in the land supply and the so-called visible hand in the Hong Kong land market has changed to become a passive role, allowing the market mechanism to work.

9.7.1 The Disadvantage of Using the Visible Hand

The use of the visible hand (i.e., as opposed to allowing market decisions) involves huge information costs to support the decisions made by government officials. In addition, there is the administrative cost of bureaucracy. Most important, the government officials do not always make correct decisions; they may often anticipate the future demand and supply incorrectly (Cheung 1983).

9.7.2 The Merits of Using the Market Mechanism (Invisible Hand) Instead of the Visible Hand

The invisible hand works more efficiently because everybody, including developers and investors, is selfish: they will try to maximise their gain and minimise their loss. Adam Smith, the father of economics, expressed his views on the invisible hand as follows: "it is only for the sake of profit that any man employs his capital… He will always, therefore, endeavour to employ it in the support of that industry of which the produce is likely to be of the greatest value, or to exchange for the greatest quantity either of money or of other goods… He is in this, as in many other cases, led by an invisible hand to promote an end which was of no part of his intention" (Smith 2000).

Competition achieves what otherwise only love can do: the divination of the innermost wishes of the other before he is aware of them. The antagonistic tension between a businessman and his competition sharpens his sensitivity to public tendencies, even to the point of clairvoyance. However, with the presence of the invisible hand, the market will automatically adjust the price to the state of Pareto optimality or efficiency (the point at which it is impossible to reallocate resources to bring one party a gain without bringing another a loss) (Wong 2000). In the past, the government intervened too extensively in the market; the day-to-day policy changes meant that the market went crazy. For example, the government announced that it would increase the land supply in its 1997 policy address; however, from March 1998, the government stopped land sales for 9 months. In 2001, the government stopped land auctions again. Later, Mr. Suen Ming Yeung, secretary for Housing, Planning and Lands, again announced that land auctions and land application would stop. All of these policy changes made it difficult for the land market or the housing market to recover; they are also evidence that government officials can never know the exact market situation. The market disarray caused by these changes is the major reason that many of us are happy to see the appearance of the Land Application Policy, which demonstrates reduced intervention in the land market. Another major effect of this policy on the land market is that it increases the opportunity cost (the highest value option forgone) of land transactions. Namely, the time costs and the transaction costs increase; this increase in the transaction costs means that the value captured in a land sale is decreased.

9.7.3 Changes in Transaction Costs

However the land application process also has shortcomings. This process has lengthened the time that it takes for the land to sell to a property developer. There is an additional half of a year added to the process. In the exchange process of a transaction, forming and operating the systems involves increasing the transaction costs. As human behaviours are complex (Li 2012a) and not everybody comply all the legal rules (Lai et al. 2007; Li 2009), there are transaction costs which include enforcement of legal contracts. Other source of transaction costs include the costs of obtaining the information (Li 2010).

9.7.3.1 Cost of Operating the System

In the past, there was no interaction between the developer and the Lands Department during the land auction or tender. The officials did not need to check the minimum price set by the developers. However, in the new system, for example, upon receipt of the application, the Lands Department will advise the applicant, in writing, as to whether the minimum price is acceptable. Reaching agreement between the parties increases the number of steps before the land auction and tender and directly increases the cost of the buyer and the seller.

9.7.3.2 Cost of Acquiring the Information

Under the old policies, the developers clearly knew the minimum price of the land in the land auction; they did not need to guess the minimum price, they only needed to value the land and to set the range that they were willing to pay based on the minimum. Under the current system, if the developer guesses incorrectly that the government has a low minimum price on the land, it might not be able to obtain the land at auction. An obvious transaction costs, as suggested by Li (2008), are the costs of knowing the product. Developers also need time to know the new "product"—a new land sale system.

9.7.3.3 Cost of Bargaining for an Agreement

Under the old policies, bargaining for an agreement was simple. For example, at a land auction, all of the parties know that their success depends on the price: the highest bidder obtains the land. However, after the introduction of the land application, the parties need to bargain for agreement before the land auction or tender.

9.7.3.4 Uncertainty in the Method of Sale

Although the applicant has indicated that they want to apply for a piece of land, they will not know the method of sale until they are informed: this creates uncertainty for the applicant and uncertainty leads to high transaction costs (Li and Li 2013). As we all know that different rules of the game may favour different people, it is undeniable that human resists change especially in times of uncertainty (Li 2012b). Developers have to know the rules of competition well because it can directly affect their ability to successfully bid for the land. The announcement of a price floor to the public makes the government land policy transparent.

Acknowledgments This chapter was originally presented as Changes from visible hand to invisible hand: Land market in Hong Kong before and after the land application system, Sixth Annual Conference of the Asian Studies Association of Hong Kong, 4–5 May 2011.

References

Cheung SNS (1983) The contractual nature of firm. J Law Econ 26(1):1–26

Chief Executive (1997) Policy programmes : the 1997 policy address. http://www.policyaddress.gov.hk/pa97/english/patext.htm

Christine Loh, Citizens Party (1997) The government high land policy: can people afford it? Citizens Party, Hong Kong

Lai LWC, Yung P, Li RYM, Ho DCW (2007) The private supply of and public demand for planning: compliance with planning conditions in the absence of direct statutory enforcement measures. Planning Pract Res 22:535–557

Lands Department (2007) Revised application procedures. http://www.landsd.gov.hk/en/images/doc/2007-1-1.pdf. Accessed 1 May 2011

Legislative Council (1997) LegCo panel on housing subcommittee on long term housing strategy review, minutes of meeting held on Wednesday, 9 April 1997, at 8:30 am in conference room B of the legislative council building. http://www.legco.gov.hk/yr96-97/english/panels/hg/lthsr/minutes/lt090497.htm. Accessed 1 May 2011

Li LH (1999) Urban reform in China. Macmillan, Hampshire

Li RYM (2008) Nature of the firm: a study on developers in China and Hong Kong. J Appl Econ Sci 3:479–486

Li RYM (2009) Achieving compliance with environmental health-related land use planning conditions in Hong Kong: perspectives from traditional motivation theories. J Environ Health 72:22–25

Li RYM (2010) Factors influencing developers' decision to sell housing units with fittings: empirical evidence from China. The University of Hong Kong, Hong Kong

Li RYM (2012a) The economics of social responsibility: the world of social enterprises. Rev Soc Econ 70:524–527

Li RYM (2012b) Relieving the aboveground land use pressure: a game theory analysis on underground space knowledge sharing. Int J Eng Ind 4:1–9

Li RYM, Li YL (2013) The relationship between law and economic growth: a paradox in China Asian. Socl Sci 9:19–30

Smith A (2000) The wealth of nations. Vintage Books, New York

Tse RYC (1993) City growth and land policy special reference to Hong Kong. Hong Kong University Press, Hong Kong

Wong YC (2000) Understanding microeconomics: HKAL/ASL

Chapter 10
An Overview of Regulations that Protect Indirect Real Estate Investors in Hong Kong During Financial Crises

Rita Yi Man Li and Yi Lut Li

Abstract All investors seek to make money. The repeated financial crises in recent years not only caused many people to lose their money; it also reminds us the importance of financial regulations to reduce investors' losses due to improper business activities in a company or stock market. Together with London and New York, Hong Kong is one of the best known financial markets in the world. Real estate investment does not rest on direct investments in hotels, residential units, or the stock market. In this decade, Real Estate Investment Trusts (REITs) and derivatives provide a new source of investment. Yet, the huge volume of transactions coupled with increasingly complicated investment tools also implies that the rules of the legal system affect many people. While many European countries and China follow civil law systems, Hong Kong follows a common law system. Judge-made law forms one of the major sources of law and lays down the important rules on indirect real estate investment. The code of practice and legislation also provide a framework for investors and entrepreneurs.

Keywords Financial crisis · Real estate investment trusts · Real estate derivative · Indirect real estate market

10.1 Introduction

Years ago, financial crisis occurred in one places usually made not much harm to other countries miles away. The first financial crisis happened in twentieth century was 1907, followed by 1921, which was more than one decade's time.

R. Y. M. Li (✉)
Sustainable Real Estate Research Center, Department of Economics and Finance, Hong Kong Shue Yan University, Hong Kong, Hong Kong SAR
e-mail: ritarec1@yahoo.com.hk

Y. L. Li
School of Law, City University of Hong Kong, Kowloon Tong, Hong Kong
e-mail: lliyilut@yahoo.com.hk

R. Y. M. Li, *Law, Economics and Finance of the Real Estate Market*, SpringerBriefs in Economics, DOI: 10.1007/978-3-642-54245-9_10,

Table 10.1 History of financial crises in the twentieth and twenty-first centuries (Li 2011a; Li and Chan 2013)

Year	Financial crisis
1907	US bank panic spread to Italy and France after the stock markets collapsed
1921	Commodity prices crashed in the US
1923	Hyperinflation in Germany started a monetary crisis
1929	"The Great Depression" began after a crash in the equity market
1931	Financial crises took place in the UK, Japan, Germany, and Austria
1933	Gold standard renounced by the US, leading to a panic in the banking system
1966	The US credit crisis led to a huge economic slump and deflation
1973	World financial crisis began after OPEC quadrupled the price of oil
1982	Global credit crunch prevented many developing countries from paying their debt
1987	Bond and equity market crashed, hitting Hong Kong and Australia's stock market badly
1989	Japanese asset bubble collapsed
1989	Junk bond crisis occurred
1992	French Maastricht Treaty sparked a crisis in the European Monetary System
1994	Major bond market correction occurred
1995	Mexican financial crisis occurred due to the Peso's pegged to the dollar during excessive inflation
1997	Asian financial crisis creates exchange rate and banking crisis, created by stock market and real estate speculation and many Asian currencies pegged to the US dollar
1998	Russia defaulted in payment obligations during the financial crisis
2000	Dot-com bubble popped in the US, creating a massive drop in equity markets from over-speculation in technology stocks
2001	Junk bond crisis occurred
2001	911 attacked. It created risk by hindering various critical communication hubs which were necessary for payment in the financial markets
2001	Economic crisis took place in Argentina, resulting in the government defaulted in various payment obligations
2002	Bond market crisis took place in Brazil
2007–date	The US real estate crisis occurred, leading to the collapse of massive international banks and financial institutions. Equity markets plummeted
2009–date	The Eurozone debt crisis occurred

Nevertheless, financial crisis in recent years occurred more frequent than before (Li 2011a). No matter what, history demonstrates that one type of periodic crisis which affects many people worldwide is financial crises. Financial crises occur locally can bring a negative impact to other parts of the world. Centuries ago, it was uncommon for local crises to affect countries miles away. Nevertheless, globalisation, international trade and the World Wide Web has shortened the distance between countries, leading to an increase in cross-border flow of GDP in the past two decades. Business cycles in East Asia have become more synchronised as a result of increasing vertical trade integration in the region. These trends provide a vivid explanation for why credit crunch problems in one local market can affect many nearby countries so quickly (Li 2011a) (Table 10.1).

10.2 Indirect Real Estate Investment Tools

An increasing number of new financial tools are being developed to enable investors to make money. Gone are the days when the stock market was the only source of indirect real estate investment. Options, swaps, accumulators and Real Estate Investment Trusts (REITs) provide alternative ways to hedge losses in the stock market or act as alternative investment tools. Due to the smaller transaction costs, the existence of a public market place in the securitized market, higher liquidity, greater number of market participants, the indirect real estate market is generally more efficient than the direct one (Oikarinen et al. 2011). The quality of financial infrastructure relies on an effective legal framework (Herring and Chatusripitak 2000), Hong Kong's success as one of the highest rank financial centers also relies on this (MacNeil and Lau 2001). History also shows that appropriate legal regulations plays an important role in financial market, for example, over-regulation and unfavourable tax treatment once resulted in a sluggish start of REITs in the U.S (Schacht and Wimschulte 2008). While previous pool of literature sheds light on causes of subprime financial crisis, few or no research paper has studied the regulations which protect indirect real estate investors. This study reviews Hong Kong's indirect real estate market statistics during financial crisis. It was found that Hong Kong REITs market's drop in prices was lowest among Australia, Japan, United Kingdom, United States, Singapore and France. The stock market ranked number two in the World during financial crisis. The chapter then proposes the reasons behind her success through the lens of well-established rules and regulations. The research results provide useful insights to legal drafters when they attempt to draft relevant rules and regulations.

The merits of including real estate in a mixed-asset portfolio have been well documented. These include liability matching characteristics and risk diversification. Nevertheless, investment in the direct real estate market, which includes retail, residential, hotel and office properties suffers from obsolescence, lumpiness information asymmetries and co-ownership problems (i.e., unclear property rights) (Hoesli and Lekander 2008). In view of these drawbacks, many investors choose to invest in the indirect real estate market, such as property stocks, derivatives and REITs.

10.2.1 Real Estate Stocks

Stock owners can be viewed as owners of the company. Although stock ownership is often raised as one of the typical examples of the principal agent problem (when the owners and managerial staff are not the same person, managers may primarily pursue selfish interests, such as power, instead of running a profitable business), it brings many benefit to both firm owners and individual investors. From entrepreneurs' perspectives, a listing in the stock market is a good source of financing.

Table 10.2 Listed property securities markets in Asia in December 2008 (Newell and Razali 2009)

Country	Number of property securities	Market capitalization (US$ billion)	% of Asia market	% of global market	World ranking (by US$)
Hong Kong	126	175	41.4	18.5	2
Japan	163	107	25.3	11.3	3
Singapore	62	39	9.2	4.1	7
China	78	56	13.2	5.9	4
India	38	16	3.8	1.7	10
Taiwan	47	6	1.4	0.6	26

Whereas borrowing money from a bank may involve huge expenses in the form of interest, money captured in the stock market does not require an expenditure on interest. On the other hand, the investors also view that it is a golden opportunity to invest in the real estate market with a small amount of money. Moreover, unlike direct real estate investment, which requires a lengthy transaction process, stocks can be bought or sold at any time.

Many of the Hong Kong listed firms are predominantly property businesses in nature, focusing on land, buildings, and estates. Many firms also conglomerate with other sectors, including trading, industrial and utility businesses, but have significant property interests on their balance sheets (Ali and Yusof 2004). Many real estate companies were listed as early as the 1970s, such as Cheung Kong Holdings, Sun Hung Kai Properties, and Sino Land. As China's economy grew quickly in the early 1990s, many China-based companies became listed in Hong Kong, such as China Overseas and China Resources.

During financial crisis, the listed property securities had not shrunk much in Hong Kong. In terms of market capitalization, Hong Kong property securities market ranked number 2 in the World (Newell and Razali 2009) (Table 10.2).

10.2.2 Real Estate Investment Trusts (REITs)

An REIT is a business trust, corporation or association which combines capital of investors to own and operate income producing real estate or to engage in real estate finance activities. REITs are analogous to mutual funds as they pool investors' funds (Daly 2008). The performance of REITs and that of the housing market are not directly comparable as the date which controls their prices come from different sources. A REIT's performance is measured in a way similar to those publicly traded stock (Monroe 2009).

In 1960, REITs were introduced in the USA to offer retail investors a possibility to invest in diversified property portfolios. A couple of countries have followed since then: Netherland (1969), Luxemburg (1988), Spain (1994), Italy (1994),

Belgium (1995), France (2003) and lately the UK (2007) (Schacht and Wimschulte 2008). There are four different types of REITS currently (Rong and Trück 2010):

1. Mortgage trusts: the assets are invested in claims where interest is the major source of income.
2. Specialized trusts: investment in development and construction which involved in sale and lease-back arrangements.
3. Hybrid trusts: the assets invest in equity and mortgages, offering an advantage which offsets the interest income against depreciation of the property.
4. Equity trusts: the assets are invested in ownerships claims to different types of properties, e.g. commercial, industrial or residential property.

There is a lot of research on REITs in overseas market. For example, He (2000) found that there is a very strong positive correlation between apartment REITs, new housing prices and stock price returns (He 2000).

In Hong Kong, the first listed in Hong Kong Stock Exchange was the Link, was launched by the Hong Kong Housing Authority in 2005 (Ooi et al. 2006). Since then, seven REITs have become listed in the Hong Kong Stock Market. To further understand the correlation between seven REITs' prices in Hong Kong, daily REITs prices data from 6 Nov 2007 to 17 June 2011 was collected from Yahoo! Finance. The Pearson correlation results from SPSS 11 show that all the seven REITs show a significant correlation with one another, i.e. most of the REITs fluctuate together. That is collapse of one REIT may affect the other REITs in market badly (Tables 10.3 and 10.4).

Fortunately, all the REITs in Hong Kong perform quite well during financial crisis. She dropped less than many other countries' REITs which include France, Japan, the U.S., Singapore, the U.K. and Australia (Table 10.5).

10.2.3 Real Estate Derivative

A "derivative" refers to an investment tool whose value is determined by, or derived from, a bundle of assets or the value of another asset. Financial derivatives can appear in a variety of forms, including futures and swaps, call and put options and more exotic complex instruments (Ong et al. 2003). Derivatives include swaps, options and so on. Many people nowadays associate derivatives with infamous financial events (e.g., the subprime financial crisis in 2007–2009) and scandals resulting from speculative use of derivative and hugely leveraged financial instruments. Joseph Stieglitz, a Nobel economics prize-winner, suggests that their use should be outlawed. Nevertheless, they are in no doubt an excellent, indispensable tool of risk management. Myron Scholes, another Nobel laureate, says a complete ban would be a luddite response which takes financial markets back decades (Suetin 2011).

The underlying assets in real estate derivative are those property related indicies, mortgage, etc. Real Estate derivatives have many uses, e.g. hedging, portfolio

Table 10.3 Real estate investment trusts in Hong Kong

Name of REIT	Hong Kong stock code	Description
The Link	823	The Link Real Estate Investment Trust was Hong Kong's first REIT. It includes a portfolio of 180 car park and retail facilities
Regal Real Estate Investment Trust	1881	Regal REIT includes a portfolio of hotel properties in Hong Kong (Enriquez 2011)
Sunlight REIT	435	Sunlight REIT includes a diversified portfolio of 8 retail and 12 office properties in Hong Kong. The retail properties are located in regional transportation hubs, new towns and other urban areas with high population density, and the office properties are located in both core and decentralised business areas (Misra 2012)
PREEF China Commercial Trusts	625	It includes Gateway Plaza, a Premium Grade A office complex located in Beijing (Chandana 2008)
Champion REIT	2778	Champion REIT owns 95.7 % of Citibank Plaza, a modern steel and glass office complex that comprises Citibank Tower, a 47-storey building, and ICBC Tower, a parking garage for 555 vehicles and a retail podium (Ali and Yusof 2004)
Prosperity REIT	808	The portfolio includes properties with direct mass transportation network access in Hong Kong. These properties include Prosperity Place, The Metropolis Tower, Prosperity Centre, Prosperity Millennia Plaza, Harbourfront Landmark, Trendy Centre and New Treasure Centre (Azhdar et al. 2010)
GZI REITs	405	Champion REIT was spun off from Great Eagle Holdings, Its principal asset includes a stake in Citibank Plaza (Ali and Ahmad 2006)

diversification or get exposure to foreign countries' real estate without buying physical property (Fabozzi et al. 2010). Real estate derivatives witness tremendously growth in the UK and Europe recently. They were introduced since the early 1980s with the establishment of the Investment Property Databank (IPD) index in the U.K (Ong and Ng 2009). Two main types of property derivatives available in the UK now are total return swaps based on IPD indices and property index certificates (Patel and Pereira 2008). In the U.S., Credit Suisse First Boston LLC teamed up with NCREIF in an attempt to create the first US real estate investment derivatives market in mid 2005 (Ong and Ng 2009).

In Asia, Hong Kong is the first city which offers real estate indexes for derivative trading. Developed jointly by GFI Colliers HK and the University of Hong Kong in November 2006, the monthly indexes cover the residential markets in Hong Kong Island, New Territories and Kowloon in Hong Kong (Ong and Ng 2009).

Table 10.4 Stock price correlations between seven REITS in Hong Kong (Author's SPSS results)

		LINK	REGAL	GZI	Prosperity	CHAMPION	SUNLIGHT	PREEF
LINK	Pearson Correlation	1	0.870(**)	0.952(**)	0.868(**)	0.817(**)	0.801(**)	0.847(**)
	Sig. (2-tailed)	.	0.000	0.000	0.000	0.000	0.000	0.000
	N	893	892	893	893	893	893	891
REGAL	Pearson Correlation	0.870(**)	1	0.924(**)	0.944(**)	0.953(**)	0.955(**)	0.889(**)
	Sig. (2-tailed)	0.000	.	0.000	0.000	0.000	0.000	0.000
	N	892	892	892	892	892	892	891
GZI	Pearson Correlation	0.952(**)	0.924(**)	1	0.907(**)	0.891(**)	0.868(**)	0.903(**)
	Sig. (2-tailed)	0.000	0.000	.	0.000	0.000	0.000	0.000
	N	893	892	893	893	893	893	891
Prosperity	Pearson Correlation	0.868(**)	0.944(**)	0.907(**)	1	0.969(**)	0.953(**)	0.854(**)
	Sig. (2-tailed)	0.000	0.000	0.000	.	0.000	0.000	0.000
	N	893	892	893	893	893	893	891
CHAMPION	Pearson Correlation	0.817(**)	0.953(**)	0.891(**)	0.969(**)	1	0.962(**)	0.863(**)
	Sig. (2-tailed)	0.000	0.000	0.000	0.000	.	0.000	0.000
	N	893	892	893	893	893	893	891
SUNLIGHT	Pearson Correlation	0.801(**)	0.955(**)	0.868(**)	0.953(**)	0.962(**)	1	0.821(**)
	Sig. (2-tailed)	0.000	0.000	0.000	0.000	0.000	.	0.000
	N	893	892	893	893	893	893	891
PREEF	Pearson Correlation	0.847(**)	0.889(**)	0.903(**)	0.854(**)	0.863(**)	0.821(**)	1
	Sig. (2-tailed)	0.000	0.000	0.000	0.000	0.000	0.000	.
	N	891	891	891	891	891	891	891

** Correlation is significant at the 0.01 level (2-tailed)

Table 10.5 Impact of financial crisis on REITs market (Newell and Razali 2009)

Countries	Impact of financial crisis on REITs market	Rank of change (least = 1, most = 7)
Hong Kong	−28.50 %	1
France	−36.80 %	2
Japan	−37.10 %	3
US	−38.30 %	4
Singapore	−56.10 %	5
UK	−59.10 %	6
Australia	−64.80 %	7
Global	−45.00 %	

10.3 Laws and Regulations that Govern Real Estate Stocks, Derivatives and REITs

Similar to many other British colonies, Hong Kong is under the umbrella of common law (Lai et al. 2007; Li 2008, 2010; Li and Poon 2009; Li and Li 2011). Financial investors are protected by legislative rules and judge-made law. Because Hong Kong was once a colony of the United Kingdom, many of these rules are rooted in UK law. Apart from that, the Basic Law also provides useful insights on financial regulations.

10.3.1 Common Law in Hong Kong: Jurisprudence and Legal Reasoning

The common law is 'common' in the sense that it is generally adopted in English terrain. Unlike the civil law system, the common law system is less influenced by Roman law. The common law system gives a great precedential weight to common law (case law), in which judges make judgments according to the doctrine of precedent of courts together with the statute statements. The court cases, however, are not restricted in local ones. Judges may also consider the overseas precedent (Li 2012). Hence, there is a wide range of variety of sources of law. Under the common law system, there are three major primary sources: statutes (laws enacted by the legislature, which is given authorisation of the government, also known as legislation), case law (judge-made law), and customary law. Alternatively, common law can be classified into two types, public and private. The former includes criminal law, administrative law and constitutional law, concerning the public bodies or officials to "protect public decision makers from risk… or challenges made by those who use judicial process as a means of political point". Private laws involve the dealings of private parties. Examples are contract and company law, which are common in indirect real estate transactions. Finally, some customs are also defined as law, i.e., customary law. Other secondary sources of law, such as directories and journals, are not treated as real law but as an interpretation.

The common law is different from the civil law system in the sense that it is part of the law which is contained in the decision of courts rather than having been enacted by the parliament. In other words, judges have to analyse the statutes (enacted by legislation), understand the overall picture of the case, then apply the various principles, with less sensible ones rendered void while more sensible ones are adopted in the judgment. If necessary, precedential judgment is also considered. The ultimate court decision will become a case law that is binding to future cases, a principle known as “stare decisis”. One should note that ‘equity’ has been incorporated into common law to provide non-monetary remedies, e.g., injunctions.

In the common law regime, jurisprudence is ‘the theoretical analysis of legal issues at the highest level of abstraction’. Therefore, jurisprudence should be understood before the discussion of common law (Manoliadis 2009). One of its important emphases is American (Legal) Realism, with O. W. Holmes (d. 1935) as its founder. This stream of academics focuses on ‘law in action’ rather than ‘law in book’. In other words, the law should be determined by practices in the real world. ‘Behind any explicit formulation of judicial reasoning there lies an implicit attitude on the part of the judge’. A judge’s personal interpretations of a case, previous case laws and statutes together affect his decision.

Because judges’ decisions influence the functioning of the law by augmenting case law, some criticisms arise. Common law is undemocratic in the sense that judges, who can alter the law, are not elected by the public. Additionally, unfairness may result because judges may be biased in particular conditions. These situations can be regarded as the drawbacks of common law (Global Times 2012). Because the jurisdiction can be influenced by the precedential judgment, legal reasoning, which is syllogistic, is involved. By comparing the statement of law (major premise) and statement of fact (minor premise), legal outcomes can be reasoned. There are three legal reasoning methods: analogy, inductive reasoning, and deductive reasoning. Analogy means that, if A has numerous similarities with B, then A and B should be similar to each other in some way. In law, similar cases should be judged in a similar way so that a similar result is obtained and thus fairness is maintained. This is also known as “stare decisis” as mentioned before. The rationale for inductive reasoning is that the court observes different cases and then works out a principle for general application of the law. Deductive reasoning means evaluating a proposition with reasoning by applying the established principles of logic. Its rationale flows from general to specific conditions.

10.4 Statues of Hong Kong Real Estate Derivatives, REITs and Stocks

Many people argue that the failure of large complex financial institutions in 2007–2009 was the results of unprepared legal and regulatory systems (Arner and Norton 2009). There is no doubt that maturity and transparency in many Asian real estate markets have improved considerably since the Asian Financial Crisis in 1997 (Ooi et al. 2006). During the global financial tsunami, Hong Kong's real estate stock and REITs perform better than many other overseas markets during financial crisis. How do Hong Kong legal rules and regulations protect investors?

10.4.1 Regulation of Real Estate Stocks

As share price equals the discounted value of expected cash flows (Nwaeze 2000; Ambrose and Bian 2010), regulations which affect the future cash flows of stock owners also play an important role in investment decisions. In Hong Kong, there are legislations which govern the property stocks trading.

Insider dealing occurs when a corporation or an individual that is directly or indirectly connected to a listed corporation uses information about that corporation to buy or sell securities with the aim to earn more than they would have without knowing this information. To ensure a level playing field for all participants in the market, the Securities (Insider Dealing) Ordinance (SIDO), and the Securities (Disclosure of Interests) Ordinance (SDIO) were implemented on September 1, 1991. Insider dealing, therefore, is a criminal offence in Hong Kong. The Insider Dealing Tribunal is empowered to impose orders to penalise insider dealers and inquire into insider dealing cases. A person who had been identified as an insider dealer may be required to pay the loss avoided by the insider dealing or an amount not exceeding the profit he/she made to the government. He/she may also be prohibited from assuming a position as a liquidator, director, manager or receiver of a company for a period of up to 5 years and/or penalised for an amount of up to three times the profit made. Any persons who contravene the orders or the investigation made by the Tribunal may be liable for a term of imprisonment of 1 year and a fine of up to $200,000. The SDIO requires the disclosure of interests for substantial directors and shareholders as well as chief executives of corporations. Regardless of where the companies are incorporated, the Ordinance is applicable to all companies listed on the Stock Exchange of Hong Kong (SEHK). A substantial shareholder is defined as anyone holding at least 5 % of the share capital of a corporation listed on the SEHK. Moreover, chief executives and directors of a listed company are obligated to declare any interest in debentures or shares in the listed company or any associated corporation and their disposal or acquisition. Any shares or debentures owned by any children under the age of 18 or spouses of directors must also be disclosed. Both substantial shareholders and directors are required to report any alterations in their interests to the SEHK within five working days. If a listed company fails to comply with the Ordinance, the officer concerned would be liable for a fine of $2,000. A further $200 fine per day must be paid in the case of continuing offences. An individual who makes a notification that is false in material particulars or who fails to make a timely notification is subject to a term of imprisonment of up to 2 years and a fine of up to $100,000 (Allame 2011).

Unlike the stock market in Japan and the US where securities law prohibits foreign securities being offered locally unless they are registered and registration is a process akin to listing on the local exchange, there is no such restriction in Hong Kong. Furthermore, Hong Kong's market is quite transparent as the authorities do not intervene in stock and bond markets via 'price-keeping operations (the Japanese broking houses may do so) or market participants try to manipulate the market for commercial or political gain (De Brouwer 2003).

10.4.2 Regulation of Real Estate Investment Trusts (REITs)

Currently, all REITs in Hong Kong are formed under Section 104 of the SFO (Chapter 571 of the Laws of Hong Kong). Some regulations control the parties that can invest in REITs. Under Section 8(2)(c) of Schedule 1, Mandatory Provident Fund Schemes (General) Regulation, a constituent fund (CF) may invest no more than one tenth of its NAV into REITs as approved by the SFC under the REIT Code. The Occupational Retirement Scheme Ordinance (**ORSO**) states that there is no explicit prohibition of SFC-authorised REIT acquisition subject to the Code on Pooled Retirement Funds (Department of Justice 2011).

On 30th July 2003, Hong Kong's final Code on Real Estate Investment Trusts was released. It permits Hong Kong REITs to be managed either externally by an external third party or internal party, i.e. parties of REIT sponsor. The manager must employ property management staff with at least 5 years experience in managing real estate and at least two officers with at least 5 years experience in managing collective investment schemes (Lockhart and Turl 2003).

The following Table 10.6 compares REITs in Hong Kong and other places. As gearing is critical for REITs to have flexibility in borrowing, a conservative approach adopted during financial crisis plays an important role in hedging against risks. Unlike the other places such as North America, Singapre and Australia where there are no limit on gearing, Hong Kong is quite conservative in setting a borrowing limit of 35 % (Wang et al. 2009).

Table 10.6 Financial regulations of REITs in Hong Kong and other places (Wang et al. 2009)

	Hong Kong	Other places
Gearing	There is borrowing limit at 35 %	There is no limit in North American, Singapore, Australia, Japan and France. In Netherland, there is no more than 60 %
Management company	At least 5 years' experience in managing property funds or employment of persons with at least 5 years	Singapore has similar requirement
Investment	restrictions	There is no restriction on overseas investment
The same principle applies in	Singapore, the U.S., Canada, the Netherlands and France	

10.4.3 Regulation of Hong Kong's Derivatives

As one of the major financial centres in the world, the emergence of derivative products has led to the question of whether Hong Kong's regulators should take the initiative in legislation reform. Partly for historical reasons, there is no single unified regulatory framework that applies to all derivative products. Hong Kong derivatives are regulated in three principal ways. The first type of regulation refers to laws that have been designed specifically for particular types of derivatives. For instance, under the Securities and Futures Ordinance (SFO), the trading of futures contracts is a regulated activity. Second, when derivatives are embedded in another investment instrument, their trading may be regulated by the regulations that are applicable to that particular instrument. For instance, a derivative may be embedded in a bond or note, such as an equity-linked note. Because an equity-linked note is regarded as a security, engaging in such derivatives trading constitute a regulated activity of securities dealing. Third, a derivative may contain certain characteristics and features similar to certain pre-existing products that have already been covered by the regulations applicable to these products; e.g., parties who are entering into longevity derivatives, credit derivatives or weather derivatives have to consider whether products as such constitute insurance. An insurance business must be regulated by the Insurance Companies Ordinance. Apart from the above-mentioned legal rules and regulations, similar to the US Commodity Exchange Act, the margin requirements and short sales restrictions of the Securities Exchange Act of 1934 which ruled out illegal speculation activities (Stout 1999), the Gambling Ordinance in Hong Kong requires the consideration of whether the derivatives issued are illegal gambling contracts (Department of Justice 2011).

10.4.4 Corporate Governance

Previous studies show that there is an ingenious connection between financial crises and investor protection. Governance variables, which include law enforcement quality and investor protection indices, are powerful predictors of the extent of market declines during a crisis. Corporate governance states the structure of responsibilities and rights among parties that have a stake in a firm. Corporate governance is often defined as a set of institutional constraints on behaviour that determine a firm's stakeholder capacities in terms of the control of cash flows and decision making within a firm. Corporate governance provides incentives for corporate insiders to protect the rights of their minority investors. The research to date on corporate governance has primarily addressed the efficacy of various mechanisms to protect shareholders from self-interested executives, and the focus has generally been on the developed Western economies. Thus, relatively little research effort has been devoted to corporate governance issues in emerging economies such as China and India. These economies, however, provide unique opportunities and challenges for governance practices and research. Well-functioning corporate governance mechanisms in emerging economies are of crucial importance for both local firms and foreign investors who are interested in pursuing the tremendous opportunities for investment and growth provided by emerging economies. From the perspective of local firms, there is evidence that firms in emerging economies (compared with their counterparts in developed countries) are discounted in financial markets because of their weak governance. As such, improvements in corporate governance can enhance investor confidence in the firms in emerging economies and can increase their access to capital. According to a 2002 McKinsey investor opinion survey, investors who were open to paying premiums were, on average, willing to pay a 25 % premium for well-governed Chinese firms and a 23 % premium for well-governed Indian firms (Li 2011b).

Corporate governance is the one of the most important legal tools for predicting investor protection. Indeed, it is also a factor that encourages the development of financial markets. When investors are well protected, they are willing to pay more for securities; corporate governance also encourages more entrepreneurs to issue securities, in turn. Shareholder and creditor protection under corporate governance includes not only the rights written into the regulations and laws but also the effectiveness of the enforcement of both. Countries that protect shareholders usually have a higher rate of initial public offering (IPO) activities, larger numbers of listed securities per capita, and more valuable stock markets than those unprotected countries (Li 2011b). The financial crisis of 1997–1998 that swept through most of East Asia countries highlighted the need for corporate governance reform in the region. There have been numerous corporate governance reform initiatives which include international and regional efforts (Cheung et al. 2007).

In Hong Kong, the three types of limited companies: private, public and listed companies are governed by the HK Companies Ordinance (the Ordinance). It was adopted from the UK Companies Acts of 1929 and 1948. The current version of the Ordinance became effective since June 1984 (Lau and Young 2006). Besides, the Stock Exchange of Hong Kong Limited published the Code on Corporate Governance Practices (the Code) and the Corporate Governance Report (CGR) in November 2004 and became became effective in 2005. Hong Kong's Corporate Governance Code requires that Non-Executive Directors have the same duties of care and skill and fiduciary duties as executive directors. The Code also shows a clear division of the responsibilities among the board's management and day-to-day management of the company's business. Whilst the board provides oversight of the process, the process of risk management involves an understanding on organizational objectives; developing programs to address the identified risks; assessing the potential impact of particular risks; and evaluating and monitoring the risks and the arrangements in place to address them. After all, risk management is essential for reducing the probability where corporate objectives will be jeopardized by unforeseen events. The board must determine the types and level of risks that are acceptable to the company, and strive to maintain risks within these levels. Internal control is one of the major means by which risk is managed (Deloitte 2013).

10.5 Conclusion

Financial crises occur periodically. The recent Eurozone debt crisis and the global subprime tsunami rooted in the United States affected many countries worldwide. Globalization, international trade and the fast growing internet services spread local financial problems quickly around the globe (Li 2011a). Real estate derivatives and REITs are new investment tools, and Hong Kong's investors and legislators are still in the discovery stage regarding these. Common law has its principles and issues and can be classified into different types and sources. It has some drawbacks as well as benefits as compared to the civil law system; for instance, it is more consistent because similar cases are given similar judgments as a result of considering the precedents of the courts. In view of these advantages and the trend of globalisation, a mix of common law and civil law systems may be observed. Besides, because REITs and derivatives are relatively new financial products, business activities as such are governed mainly by rules that are applied to other similar products in Hong Kong. The subprime financial crisis, however, underscored the importance of appropriate regulations. It is expected that regulations will be designed specifically for these tools.

Acknowledgments This chapter is a revised version of a paper published in Li RYM, Li YL (2011) An overview of regulations that protect real estate stocks, REITs and derivative investors in Hong Kong, Lex Et Sciential Economic Series, vol 18, No 2, pp 200–211. The author would like to thank the publisher for agreeing to republish.

References

Ali HM, Ahmad NH (2006) Knowledge management in Malaysian banks: a new paradigm. J Knowl Manage Pract 7

Ali HM, Yusof ZM (2004) Knowledge management in Malaysian banks: a study of causes and effects. J Inf Dev 20:161–168

Allame SM (2011) Effect of organizational culture on success of knowledge management system's implementation (case study: Saderat bank in Isfahan province). Interdisc J Contemp Res Bus 2:321–346

Ambrose W, Bian X (2010) Stock market information and REIT earnings management. J Real Estate Res 32:101–137

Arner DW, Norton JJ (2009) Building a framework to address failure of complex global financial institutions. Hong Kong Law J 39:95–128

Azhdar K, Ebrahim G, Fatemeh N, Samaneh M (2010) Customer knowledge management in the Iranian banks: an empirical research. EuroJournals 9:74–91

Chandana G (2008) Knowledge management in India : a case study of an Indian bank. J Nepalese Bus Stud 1:37–49

Cheung YL, Thomas Connelly J, Limpaphayom P, Zhou L (2007) Do investors really value corporate governance? Evidence from the Hong Kong market. J Int Financ Manage Acc 18:86–122

Daly WJ (2008) Germany and the United Kingdom: will those markets experience the same success as the United States. Transnatl Law Contemp Probl 17:839–868

De Brouwer G (2003) Financial markets, institutions, and integration in East Asia. Asian Econ Pap 2:53–80

Deloitte (2013) Overview of corporate governance (Hong Kong SAR). http://www.corpgov.deloitte.com/site/ChinaEng/hongkong-governance-profile/. Accessed 11 June 2013

Department of Justice (2011) Bilingual laws information system. http://www.legislation.gov.hk/index.htm. Accessed 21 June 2011

Enriquez JG (2011) Tug-o-where: situating mobilities of learning (t)here. Learn Media Technol 36:39–53

Fabozzi FJ, Shiller RJ, Tunaru RS (2010) Property derivatives for managing European real-estate risk. Eur Financ Manage 16:8–26

Global Times (2012) Ningbo people does not win. China is the loser (In Chinese). http://view.news.qq.com/a/20121029/000011.htm. Accessed 29 Oct 2012

He LT (2000) Causal relationships between apartment REIT stock returns and unsecuritized residential real estate. J Real Estate Portfolio Manage 6:365–372

Herring RJ, Chatusripitak N (2000) The case of the missing market: The bond market and why it matters for financial development. ADB Institute Working Paper

Hoesli M, Lekander J (2008) Real estate portfolio strategy and product innovation in Europe. J Prop Invest Financ 26:162–176

Lai LWC, Yung P, Li RYM, Ho DCW (2007) The private supply of and public demand for planning: compliance with planning conditions in the absence of direct statutory enforcement measures. Plann Pract Res 22:535–557

Lau AKL, Young A (2006) Corporate governance in Hong Kong: 'the state of affairs'. Compliance Regul J 1:39–48

Li RYM (2008) Nature of the firm: a study on developers in China and Hong Kong. J Appl Econ Sci 3:479–486

Li RYM (2010) A study on the impact of culture, economic, history and legal systems which affect the provisions of fittings by residential developers in Boston, Hong Kong and Nanjing. Int J Glob Bus Manage Res 1:131–141

Li RYM (2011a) The importance of corporate governance in Hedging against global financial crisis in the future India. Creating a better India through corporate governance conference, India

Li RYM (2011b) The importance of corporate governance in Hedging against global financial crisis in the future india. Creating a better India through corproate governance conference, Sri Ganganagar, Rajasthan, India
Li RYM (2012) The internalization of environmental externalities affecting dwellings: a review of court cases in Hong Kong. Econ Aff 32:81–87
Li RYM, Chan HY (2013) The impact of Eurozone debt crisis on China's property and land market. European Union Studies Association Asia Pacific Conference, Macau
Li RYM, Li YL (2011) Judges' view on the price of environmental externalities in the United Kingdom. US–China Law Rev 8:994–1007
Li RYM, Poon SW (2009) Workers' compensation for non-fatal construction accidents: review of Hong Kong court cases. Asian Soc Sci 5:15–24
Lockhart D, Turl G (2003) Reits: success in Hong Kong depends on flexible regulation. Int Financ Law Rev 22:13–14
MacNeil I, Lau A (2001) International corporate regulation: listing rules and overseas companies. Int Comp Law Q 50(787):802–803
Manoliadis O (2009) Education for sustainability: experiences from Greece. J Prof Issues Eng Educ Pract 135:70–74
Misra PK (2012) Each-one-teach-one mobile networks: an innovative strategy for knowledge access in Asian countries. Educ Media Int 49:109–122
Monroe P (2009) REITs amidst the current real estate crisis: an analysis of the REITs investment diversification and empowerment act. J Bus Secur Law 9:239–260
Newell G, Razali MN (2009) The impact of the global financial crisis on commercial property investment in Asia. Pacific Rim Prop Res J 15:430–452
Nwaeze ET (2000) Positive and negative earnings surprises, regulatory climate, and stock returns. Contemp Acc Res 17:107–134
Oikarinen E, Hoesli M, Serrano C (2011) The long-run dynamics between direct and securitized real estate. J Real Estate Res 33:73–104
Ong SE, Ho KHD, Lim CH (2003) A constant-quality price index for resale public housing flats in Singapore. Urban Stud 40:2705–2729
Ong SE, Ng KH (2009) Developing the real estate derivative market for Singapore: issues and challenges. J Prop Invest Financ 27:425–432
Ooi JTL, Newell G, Sing TF (2006) The growth of REIT markets in Asia. J Real Estate Lit 14(203–204):206–222
Patel K, Pereira R (2008) Pricing property index linked swaps with counterparty default risk. J Real Estate Financ Econ 36:5–21
Rong N, Trück S (2010) Returns of REITS and stock markets. J Prop Invest Financ 28:34–57
Stout LA (1999) Why the law hates speculators: regulation and private ordering in the market for OTC derivatives. Duke Law J 48:701–782
Suetin A (2011) Post-crisis developments in international financial markets. Int J Law Manage 53:51–61
Schacht Ulrich, Wimschulte Jens (2008) German property investment vehicles and the introduction of G-REITs: an analysis. J Prop Invest Financ 26:232–246
Wang H, Sun Y, Chen Y (2009) Special considerations for designing pilot REITs in China. J Prop Invest Financ 27:140–161

MIX
Papier aus verantwortungsvollen Quellen
Paper from responsible sources
FSC® C105338

If you have any concerns about our products,
you can contact us on
ProductSafety@springernature.com

In case Publisher is established outside the EU,
the EU authorized representative is:
Springer Nature Customer Service Center GmbH
Europaplatz 3, 69115 Heidelberg, Germany

Printed by Libri Plureos GmbH
in Hamburg, Germany